HOW TO BREAK 10 COMMON CHILDHOOD MYTHS

DIANE & CHAD FINKBEINER

Copyright © 2011 F2 Distributing
All rights reserved.
ISBN-13: 978-0615436210

DEDICATED WITH LOVE TO

F2

SF

TLG

our family and friends

CONTENTS

Introduction   I

Myth 1   **No Means Yes**   1
Parents will learn the importance of the word "No"
actually meaning "No" and how that encourages their
children to be productive.

Myth 2   **Responsibility, What's That?**   22
We will discuss the abilities of children to handle all kinds
of responsibilities that will make their futures much
brighter.

Myth 3   **Pouting, Whining and Crying Always Works**   42
We will discuss the different levels of pouting, whining,
and crying at all ages and give suggestions to help curb
that behavior.

Myth 4   **Manners are for Geeks**   61
Manners have always been a key to higher socialization
skills. These skills will help shape children and their
futures as they mature and grow.

Myth 5   **I Am the King of the Castle**   79
If you feel like the outsider in your child's room, let us give
you some pointers in reminding them just whose room it
really is.

Myth 6	**They'll Fix It for Me**	93
	Teaching your child to be responsible is the basis for becoming a productive member of society rather than being crippled with lack of independence in the future.	
Myth 7	**It's Never My Fault**	109
	We will discuss the "It's never my fault" syndrome and what to do to minimize its frequency.	
Myth 8	**Everybody Does It**	127
	We have all been exposed to "Everybody Does It," but the time has come to show your children, and maybe yourself, just how little it works in the real world.	
Myth 9	**Don't Worry, They'll Say It Again**	146
	If you constantly repeat yourself and think your children must be hard of hearing, now is the time to show them just what society's actual response is to ignoring someone.	
Myth 10	**I Hate Family Time**	163
	Do your children really hate family time, or just what it has become? We will discuss some new techniques to engage them in enjoyable family time.	

SPECIAL THANKS TO

Scott, Lauren, Shannon,

Foster, Linda, Jim, Ames

&

Editor Elizabeth Ridley

INTRODUCTION

DIANE:

When I was a little girl, I loved school—papers, pencils, coloring, reading—what's not to love? My third grade teacher, Miss Sally, loved us, and it showed. At the end of the school year, she gave us each a journal to take home in which she had written a personalized inscription. Wow!! From that time on, I wanted to be a teacher just like Miss Sally…and I think I became exactly that. I loved the kids; I loved inventing new lessons; I loved seeing the light shine in their eyes when they finally understood.

My husband, Fred, and I began teaching in 1968; one in the junior high, the other in the elementary school. We both soon decided that "Do What's Best for Kids" would be our motto. While we taught "subjects," we also tried to instill traits in the children that would help them grow into responsible, independent young adults. After ten years of teaching, we decided to start our own family, which resulted in two great boys: Chad and Scott. We used many of our teaching techniques, and of course many other methods, to help our boys grow into the thoughtful, caring, responsible men they are now. When Fred died in 1996, the strength that had been instilled in all of us carried us through. We wish to help parents learn the techniques and tips that will produce the great adults that our future needs.

I learned many things as a result of the history of my teaching career. After teaching for fifteen years in first and second grades, I was transferred to a junior high to teach math to seventh and eighth graders. Yow! Panic! All summer I was totally terrified of the idea of those "big guys." When I actually began the year…surprise, surprise! The kids were really just taller, goofier, and sweeter second graders. After six years there, I volunteered to go back to the elementary, where I taught sixth grade for eleven years. Then, I finally decided to shake myself up and I began teaching second grade again, where I reinforced the idea that kids of all ages are the same. I was amazed at the things they all seemed to believe and how those beliefs contributed to their actions.

I taught for 41 years because I always loved it, but the

kids and society in general did a lot of changing. In "the old days," all but the most hardened child had respect for teachers and school because it was required at home. I could spend all my time teaching the curriculum and finding creative ways to do so. As time went on, more of the children brought "attitudes" to school with them. I taught them how to behave appropriately in school and then taught the curriculum. Near the end of my career, I felt I needed to teach the children how to interact with each other and with adults, and I often needed to "teach" the parents how to improve the behavior of the kids after being requested to help.

I began to make a list of "myths" that most children seem to believe about how life works. I called them chapters and laughingly decided they would make great ideas for a book I would eventually write. I put that legal pad away in a file cabinet after telling some friends and family about these confusing issues for children, some of which you'll see in this book: "No Means Yes," "Responsibility, What's That?," "Don't Worry; They'll Say It Again," and seven other myths.

When I changed classrooms four years later, there it was again…the "myth" list, and just as true as it had been. My older son Chad had just begun teaching eighth grade after spending time subbing in high schools. He mentioned the legal pad list of childhood beliefs that he had seen years earlier, and wondered if I still had it. When I showed him, he was flabbergasted. Sure enough, it was true in his classrooms also.

Therein began the process of the two of us preparing and presenting parenting and teaching workshops and writing a book called "How to Break 10 Common Childhood Myths" to help parents.

When I decided to leave teaching, it was very hard for me …who was I? Who would I become now? I'm hoping that in the future, through workshops and books, Chad and I can help more parents and teachers in their quest to raise responsible, independent young adults. I believe children learn most of their important life lessons based on experiences in their family life. We hope the stories of our family can be used to help your family now.

CHAD:

As a kid, I always liked school, but mostly because it was a chance for me to see my friends. I was a good student and did well in school, but it was never my passion...recess was! I loved recess and gym class and wood shop—all of the classes in which you were active and moving around. Growing up I had a lot of great teachers who taught me all kinds of interesting things, but the education I gained from the playground suited me better. During my senior year of high school, my dad passed away; it was the most difficult portion of my life. I felt lost, like I didn't know what to do or whom to become. My plan had been to go to Central Michigan and become a teacher, but my outlook on life had changed in an instant. I had caught a glimpse of just how short life could be, and I never wanted to take another second for granted. "Carpe Diem" became my motto. When I got to CMU, I began taking my educational classes and although they were interesting, they weren't exciting to me. That is when I found the recreation, parks, and leisure services department! Recreation was perfect for me; it provided the excitement and adventure that I had been searching to find.

Throughout the four years I was studying at Central, I worked as a ski instructor at Boyne Highlands on the weekends to feed my adrenaline rush. It was everything I had ever hoped for: adventure, excitement, outdoors, and challenging. Being a ski instructor was the most amazing job in the world; not only did I get to teach people a useful skill, but I got to do what I loved most for a living. After working my way up from the "Kids Camp" all the way to private requested lessons, I knew that I had found my calling. I pursued a Commercial Recreation degree with new determination, knowing that I had finally found the path I was looking for.

When I graduated from Central, I moved to Breckenridge, Colorado, to pursue my dream of becoming a ski school director out west. I packed everything I owned into a 1991 Bronco, and headed west to fulfill my dreams. I lived in Breck at the base of Peak 8 for one year. It was the greatest year of my life. I met amazing friends, worked my ideal job, and started living the life I thought was meant for me! My ski instructor paycheck just barely covered my housing, and to make ends meet I started working at The Village Hotel as a bellman. Life was great; I had good friends, a steady job, and just enough income to keep me happy, but all that was about to change. One fateful day while I was backcountry riding, I hyper-extended my knee and heard a "pop." It was a torn ACL and my ski instructing days were over. About this same time, my lease was up and many of my friends were moving back home to "start their real lives." I had a decision to make, and I decided to move back home for physical therapy on my knee before setting out on my next grand adventure.

During physical therapy, I needed a job to help pay for miscellaneous expenses. To be honest, I really just needed money to be able to go out with my friends whom I hadn't seen in a year. Since I had already completed 90 credit hours of college-level courses, I was eligible to substitute teach in my Mom's district. I began subbing and LOVED IT! I loved everything about it; the kids were great (most of the time), the hours were phenomenal, and the job changed every day, giving me the challenge that I crave. I decided to go back to school and get my teaching degree. So there I was back in school again, starting over. I attended Baker College for the next three years while subbing on the side. Once I graduated from Baker, I was lucky enough to be hired into Armada Schools as an eighth grade history and English teacher.

My first year teaching was a disaster! The students challenged everything—they didn't participate in class; didn't listen to directions; they certainly didn't finish their homework. Nothing I learned in school prepared me for the job of disciplining students for more than one day at a time. When I was subbing, even if it was a terrible day, I knew that the next day I would be somewhere else. But now that I had my own classroom I needed to know how I would fix it the next day. I did a lot of venting to my Mom about the problems I was having in the classroom. She told me that much of what I was seeing in the middle school coincided with what she was seeing in the elementary. I mentioned to her the book chapters that I had seen years earlier and we began looking at them more closely to see if there was a rational solution. And so began our mission: to help parents and teachers not only to understand their children, but to help them succeed in the raising of those children to grow up to be respectful, productive members of society. In the years since, my classroom experience has improved tenfold, and the methods and techniques discussed in this book are based on my real-life experiences with their implementation.

Our greatest hope is that this book may act as a source of inspiration—the spark you need to make the changes you see necessary for a lifetime of happiness with your children—because they're worth it!

MYTH 1
NO MEANS YES

There was a time not long ago when the word "no" actually meant "no." There was no arguing, no whining, and no chance that the word of someone in a position of authority would be challenged. So what has happened in the recent past to bring about this change in ideology all so often seen in the local grocery store? There is a better question. "What can be done in the near future to bring this change back within check?" Children in today's society have a new and often unrestricted freedom of… well, freedom of everything that adults have earned through time and wisdom. There are many ways to rear children and fortunately for society, no one solution is right for every child. However, there are universal truths when dealing with children that allow parents and teachers to help guide while encouraging productive growth. Even parents who aren't good at making sure that

NO means NO still set certain boundaries involving the street, electrical outlets, etc. Your children know now that there are some important boundaries for you; their young minds begin trying to figure out which ones are truly important and which ones they can ignore. In fact, all of the boundaries should be important if they are coming from you. Through years of research and observation, we have begun to see, organize, and utilize the following truths:

1. Work backwards from today: When did your children begin to believe that they were the ones in control?

2. "Do this" is much more effective than "Don't do that."

3. As a parent or teacher you must interact—get off the couch and on your feet.

4. "No" must always mean "no" and it must mean "no" forever, without exception: The word you are probably searching for is "maybe"… "maybe" can lead to "yes" in time.

5. Children are not allowed to question your decisions without first agreeing to the terms.

6. You are not your children's best friend—you are their guide and protector for life.

7. Children need, and actually appreciate, boundaries—use them to your advantage.

8. "Hating" you now will lead to love and respect later.

9. Children should believe that any punishment is possible.

10. Children should not be afraid of their parents, but they should be afraid of their punishments.

11. Threats work…use them!

12. Don't discipline in anger, but if you do, explain your actions to the child.

1. Parenting, as well as teaching, is based on understanding the mindset of a child. Children learn, think, and react much differently than adults; however, if you are reading a book about child rearing, you already know this, don't you?! What you need to do now is step back and take an objective look at your family and what it is that you would like to see change. Figure out when you allowed your children to believe that they were the ones calling the shots. Make a list of all the things you would like to see change in your relationship with your child, or the things you would find in your ideal relationship. Once this list is complete you can begin making it a reality—it just takes a little work and a lot of patience.

2. The key to regaining the "control" that is lacking in today's world is proximity-based relationships. The most effective way to "guide" your child is to physically be there to guide them. Trust and respect is earned over time and must be deliberately taught. When children are young, it makes sense to be by their side, but as they grow up we, as adults, believe that we no longer need to be there by their side. Unfortunately, when we leave their side physically, we often leave their side emotionally and intellectually as well, forcing the child to learn from their peers—other

children who are just as confused and immature as they are.

> **DIANE:** *We lived on a little man-made lake when our boys were growing up. Many people asked us if we were worried about raising our kids near a lake. Did we worry that they may fall in and drown? Of course, they always had "floaties" or life vests when playing in the lake, but more importantly, when they were young they never went outside without us.*
>
> *This was partially because of their safety but also because we wanted to have fun with our boys every chance we could, which would allow us to be a close-knit family. In order to keep an eye on our boys, my husband and I had the kids around us all the time. If they went outside to play when they were young, we went with them. Because it was just what we did as a family, they never thought it strange that we spent so much time together.*

3. Get off that couch and get back into their lives. Your "couch" is anything that may be keeping you from paying attention to your child. Our world is so full of distractions

keeping parents and teachers from truly connecting with the children in their lives: long hours at work, television in every room, iPods, and cell phones, to name just a few. It is even more important to make those personal connections in spite of the hustle and bustle of a modern, technology-driven world. Children need directed teaching from parents to show them what they should do instead of yelling "no" over and over again.

> **DIANE:** *The advantage of using physical activity to engage your child will amaze you. When Chad and Scott were very young, I spent much of my time following them around with my eyes and then, if necessary, with my feet. When kids are little, their job is to explore and discover boundaries. I loved watching them learn: what an end table handle felt like, how the material on the couch was different from the material on the floor, what you could see out a window.*
>
> *But, because I watched them a lot, I could often tell when they were curious about something dangerous like a cord, an outlet, or a piece of a plant. When my voice started saying, "No, no, Honey," my feet were already headed that direction to help divert their*

attention to something else. The actual physical activity of redirecting them helped in more than one way.

My interaction with them became a lifelong one, always being concerned and aware. Some would say over-protective, but I didn't care. The idea of "No," even when said in a calm, quiet voice became a serious idea, not to be debated.

4. You've seen it a thousand times: you're walking through the grocery store and there they are: a woman with a half-full shopping cart staring at the recent text message she has received, dragging her young child behind her while he is stumbling and dragging his feet as they pass the all-too-familiar toy aisle.

SCENARIO 1: You are in the grocery store with Joey. Pushing the cart through the aisles, you look for the items on your list while Joey snoops at everything on the lowest shelf. All of a sudden Joey yells, "Mom! Look! Can I get this… I've wanted it forever! Can I get it? Can I? Can I?"
Of course that toy is not on your list at the moment, so you say, "No!"
"But, Mom!"

"No, Joey!"

"Mom, I'll never ask for anything ever again...puhleeeze?"

"Joey, stop it!"

Then the embarrassment sets in: "You are SOO mean, you never do anything for me—it's not fair!"

As you notice the other customers in the store staring at you, you mutter to Joey in an angry tone, "FINE!! Get your toy and let's go!!"

What has this mother just taught her young son? The boy has learned that if he is obnoxious enough, Mom will give in and he will get what he wants. This is one of those universal truths we were talking about earlier…remember a guy by the name of Pavlov? Children need to know that when you say the word "NO," you mean it and no matter what else happens, that "no" will not change to a "yes" under any circumstances. Most of the time parents and teachers say "no" when they really mean "maybe" because it's a snap judgment and because it comes easy. The word "maybe" is your best friend; it gives you time to think. Anytime you need to decide what the answer should be, "maybe" is the way to go. Having a predetermined response to what you know is going to be a question you hear is even better.

SCENARIO 2: On the way to that same grocery store, you and Joey have a conversation. You say, "Joey, remember this shopping trip today is for grocery items on my list. I won't be buying anything extra. Do you think you could help me use my coupons today and find some of the stuff for the cart?" In the store, Joey sees the same toy and asks the same question, but the tone is different because of your talk in the car.

"Hey, Mom, could I maybe get this toy...it's my favorite?"

You reply, "Sweetie, not this time...but you can go pick out your favorite cereal today instead of our usual corn flakes if you want."

Redirecting attention onto something else is usually your best defense. If that tends not to work with your child, though, you could also try, "If you really like it you could see if you have enough allowance money at home, and we can come back tomorrow to get it with your own money."

What did your child learn this time? First, that no really does mean no. Second, that you have the power in the relationship, and third, that you can have a friendly and respectful discussion with your child even if you have differing wants. Then, smile...parenting, teaching, and guiding can all be fun and full of smiles. It's your tone that says more than your words—try to de-escalate the situation by making the child see that you are not mad or unreasonable-simply making a decision and sticking with it.

5. In order to ensure that the children are listening to you and understand that the adult is in charge, the child should never be allowed to argue, question, or dispute a "no" answer to any question without first agreeing that the answer is indeed, "No." Children should, however, be allowed to ask why the answer is a "No." When Mommy tells the child that he cannot have the toy this time, the only acceptable response should be, "Ok, but can I ask why?" This dialogue shows that the parent is in control and the answer is not going to change, but the child can be curious as to why he is not getting what it is he thinks he should be getting. Your child's concern should be valued, and you can let him know that you feel this way by ending the conversation with, "I understand that you're upset and I'm sorry, but you'll have a chance to get one next time if you can show me that you are a big boy who deserves a reward." Even a small reward is enough to help illustrate your "deal."

CHAD: *As a kid, one of my favorite toys was Matchbox cars. There was an almost infinite array of different* *cars, and the best part about them was that they were very inexpensive. When I was growing up, these toys were less than one dollar apiece. When I was told I was being good and could pick out a small toy from the toy aisle, I almost always chose a Matchbox car. I knew the difference between a small reward toy from the grocery store and an expensive birthday present toy from Toys R Us. Children have to be taught what you expect from them, and they must learn to follow the examples as they have been set. If I had showed up from the toy aisle with a technical Lego set that cost more than a couple of dollars, I knew that my Mom would tell me to put it back and I would NOT be allowed to grab another one—being greedy was not tolerated in our family. This intolerance helped me to appreciate all that I was given.*

6. You have friends, and family, acquaintances, and mentors in your life; the key to the success of raising kids, be it as a parent or as a teacher, is to know where you fall within this spectrum. You are your child's mentor and protector for their entire lives, and trying to be their best friend takes this ability away from you. As teachers, we

hear so many stories about parents who try to be "the cool parents." These "mentors" have lost their way by trying to be friends with their kids and their kids' friends. This is the house that usually allows kids to drink and smoke at a young age because that is what the kids want. The parents' excuse is that it is safer to have the kids do this at a house where there is supervision, but what they are actually doing is setting an example of irresponsibility for their children and those near to them. What are they teaching? That rules and boundaries do not apply to everyone. Being your child's friend takes away your power to be able to guide and protect them.

> **CHAD:** *My first year of teaching, I spent most of my time trying to show the kids in my eighth grade class that they could trust me; that I was there to help them; that I was their friend. It was the hardest year of my life because once the students actually believed that I was their friend, my ability to use my authority was gone. After all, do you always do everything your friends tell you to do? Over the course of the following two years, I began to assert myself as someone that they could trust; someone who was there to help them; someone they should*

see as a mentor and protector...not as a friend. Being fair but firm made all the difference. The next two years were amazing. I made the kind of connections with students that I had strived for during that first year; however, I was also able to retain the control that was mandatory for a teacher to have. Kids want boundaries, whether they are willing to admit it or not.

7. For as much as they protest, children want and need boundaries. As we just stated, if you are trying to be the child's friend you are unable to fully support their maturation process. Parents who focus on being friends with their children are indulging the selfish portion of their natural need to be accepted. It's amazing how often you see people allowing children to manipulate them in order to gain acceptance from that child (who will end up resenting that person in the long run). Parents need to be okay with knowing that children will dislike many of the decisions imposed upon them, but if the parent remains steadfast, the rewards and acceptance will be tenfold after the child grows up. Clearly defined boundaries give children a sense of belonging; they know what is and is not expected of them, and this allows them to focus on

being good versus testing boundaries.

> **DIANE:** *How many times in your child's life do you think you'll hear him say, "But so-and-so can do it!"? You'll hear it many more times if you cave in when they're young or if you try to be their friend by agreeing to something you know you shouldn't. Our boys knew that when friends came to our house, our rules remained the same. If Bobby started to throw toys, whether his Mom was there or not, the toys would be taken away. Bobby might complain to us or to his Mom, or his Mom might say, "Oh, he didn't mean to...", but we would still say, "I'm sorry, but we don't throw toys in this house...why don't you guys go grab a snack or something?" We would use the redirecting method so there was no anger or embarrassment, but we had not backed down on the boundaries we wanted our children to have. Try to remember what's best for the child's future instead of any instant gratification you might get from backing down.*

8. When setting the boundaries for your children, you will undoubtedly run into much resistance from them. Their job is to test the boundaries that you provide; your

job is to stand firm on those boundaries to prove that you love them enough to protect them. At some point your children will probably say, either with their words or their eyes, that they hate you. It is hard to hear the ones you love most resenting you, but you need to know that they are only lashing out and don't really mean the words the way the adult mind understands them. It is just their way of pushing back on the boundary. You probably won't hear from them that they understood how you raised them until they are fully grown, but in time they will tell you that they appreciated the boundaries that you set forth when they were young.

CHAD: *It wasn't until my Mom and I started working on this book that I was actually able to vocalize to her that I truly appreciated how I was raised. As a kid, I hated that my parents were so overprotective, and they knew that I hated that. As I grew up, I began to understand why they were that way. After more time passed, I began not only to understand but appreciate the way I was raised. It's not something that usually comes up in conversation, though; I found out during the creation of this series that my Mom never really knew if Scott and I ever* *understood why we were kept from doing certain things growing up. Your children are probably not going to thank you for the work you put into their upbringing until they are much older. In fact, it probably won't be until they are raising kids of their own, but that doesn't mean that they don't appreciate and love what you do for them. When you put their interests first, you will be rewarded in the long run with children who grow up to be everything you hoped and dreamed for.*

9. How do you set boundaries? Usually with punishments and rewards—the same way you would train a puppy. Only this puppy will outlive you and will never truly run away from home. Punishments should never be the same; you should always change your position based on the situation. The most important part about negative reinforcement is that your child should honestly believe that ANY punishment is possible. No matter how outlandish or how ridiculous, the child should believe, in their hearts, that the parent or teacher is capable of enforcing whatever it is that they want.

DIANE: *In a fifth-grade classroom, a special pen turned up missing. I asked if anyone had seen it and* *if so, to just return it since I was sure it was just an accident. I focused in on the guilty party (yes, I did know), stared hard, and then looked all around the room. I said, "I wonder what the punishment might be for not only taking something but then also lying about it?...Hmmm, probably not good...I'll try one more time...anyone want to return something that accidentally might have fallen in the wrong place?" The "someone" did return the pen and we all returned to our work. I quietly then took the child to the hallway for a one-on-one reality check. He knew that I knew. He also knew that another sort of consequence would be very possible in the future. Uncertainty leads to nervousness and anxiety about what they have done, which is good for reminding kids to follow the rules.*

10. Making sure that children do not associate punishment with the authority figure, but instead with the action that led to the punishment, is essential. The last thing you want to do is make children afraid of you. Trust, respect, positive ideology: all are impossible in the presence of fear. If your children fear you, the only reaction that you are able to facilitate from them is fight

or flight. Once a child disassociates the punishment from the person enforcing the punishment, that child is able to learn from the mistake and grow. That said, children SHOULD be afraid of the punishments that you may enforce, although a "look" should be enough to stop them in their tracks. A healthy fear of consequences is what keeps most responsible people from indulging their every whim. This same fear is what will keep your child or student on track. There will always be consequences for your actions. If they do not learn the concept of consequences when they are young, they WILL learn it from the police and society later.

DIANE: *Whenever you see a television program or a movie that involves abuse of some sort, what kind of look do you see on the face of the abused? What about on the face of the abuser? Do you ever want your child to see that look on your face? Do you ever want to see that petrified look on your child's face? That is what happens when you punish out of anger—you lose all control. Your position of authority changes to one of force. Shouting is also a loss of control; you shouldn't have to browbeat your own child. If your child learns that your "game* *face" means what it says, then the face doesn't have to be an angry one, just a serious one, under complete control. When the boys were little, we had to remember to have them look at us each time we talked to them. They needed to know the difference in the looks we gave them. Was this the "silly, let's have fun" look? Okay, lots of acceptable responses for that one. Was this the "serious, game face?" Uh, oh...the only response to that one is to pay attention and listen carefully to what comes next.*

11. Now that your children are afraid of your punishments and they believe that anything is possible, it is time to put their imaginations to work for you. Threats are a very effective and essential part of parenting. The change that we encourage parents and teachers to implement is a philosophy of less information being more effective. Timelines should not be given and information should be kept to a minimum. If I know that I only have to go without my cell phone or my Legos for a week, I can wrap my head around that and get through it without internalizing why I had them taken away in the first place. If you don't tell the child how long they will be without whatever it is that they value most, and they also know

that they aren't allowed to ask when they will be getting it back unless they want to increase that time, the chances that they will misbehave are greatly decreased.

CHAD: *When I was a kid, I never knew what my punishment would be, nor for how long I would be punished. On the rare occasion that I did get in trouble and got "grounded," I was never told for how long (even when I made a point to ask). I was told that I was grounded until I learned my lesson, and if I asked again when I was "ungrounded" the time would only increase. I would hear my friends say, "I'm grounded for the weekend," and all I could think was, "that's not that long…I'd be happy with just a weekend." Even though most times I was grounded for no more than three days, I knew in my heart that it could be three weeks if my behavior didn't improve. Because I was under the impression that my grounding could last forever, my behavior improved much more quickly than the behavior of my friends who knew they only had to endure one weekend of discipline.*

12. After all this talk about discipline and punishment, we have to tell you the one thing that makes it much

harder—never discipline in anger! Okay, now that you are done chuckling—because let's face it, you know you are going to at some point or another. When that time comes, it is important to explain to your child why you punished him in order to maintain his trust. It is important not to discipline when you are angry because it lets the child know that you are not in control. Once they see that you are out of control, it gives them the power. You must always remain strong, cool, and composed if you want your child to believe that you are always right.

MYTH 2

RESPONSIBILITY - WHAT'S THAT?

The lack of responsibility in America today is an epidemic, and the most prevalent place to see this trend is the public school system. Children today have grown up under the assumption that it is all right to be irresponsible and downright lazy. Constantly counting on parents and teachers to bail them out of situations is not only harmful to the child's upbringing, but also harmful to their self-esteem. "Forgetting" seems to be the most common phrasing for irresponsibility; however, it is not really forgetting that they are doing. What they are doing instead is choosing not to do something that takes more effort because they believe that it will be taken care of for them. "My parents will always be there to take care of me" is a dangerous concept that kids feed off of and parents guilt themselves into believing. In order to ensure that children grow up to be productive and responsible members of society, they will need to learn a few of these important lessons:

1. When you tell your children to do something, they WILL comply...voluntarily or kicking and screaming.

2. A defiant "NO" or a tongue stuck out equals punishment, without hesitation.

3. How far are you willing to go now to give your child a good future?

4. You must be willing to take things away; -- permanently, if necessary.

5. A self-sufficient adult is our goal—do not bail your child out unless you are willing to do so until he is 40!

6. Make them responsible for their own homework, lunches, field trip notes, etc.

7. There are, and always will be, consequences for forgetting.

8. Show caution when using the computer or other forms of technology.

9. Check up on your children—call them out when you catch them being untruthful.

10. Your child not knowing what you are capable of is your greatest asset.

11. Be okay with letting your child use you as an excuse.

12. "Game face and personal space."

1. Especially when children are young, they need to know that they are not in charge and that you as the adult will be the one making the decisions. When a child understands that he is required to comply, it takes the availability of being defiant completely away. As children get older, they are going to begin to push back on the rules you set forth for them, which is why it's so important to establish the boundaries early on. This is not only important for a healthy relationship between parent and child, but it is also vitally important for safety reasons that children do what they are told when they are told to do it.

CHAD: *When I was a very young child, we had an electric coil-style heater that would glow bright orange when it was in operation. I remember being told not to play with the heater, and every time I came too close to it, I remember hearing the urgency in my parents' voices. One day I was all alone in the family room while my parents were in the garage and in the kitchen. I couldn't help myself—I reached through the protector bars and touched the heater coil. I'm not sure I had ever screamed so loudly in my life. My mom came running down the stairs and tried to find out what had happened. I had a second-degree burn on the tip of my finger and* *couldn't stop crying. I had to learn the hard way that listening to my parents was in my best interest. Tell your kids why you are so adamant about your boundaries, and they will not need to challenge those boundaries as often.*

2. Any behavior that can be deemed disrespectful or rude should be punished without hesitation! The concept of respect has been in stark decline for the past few decades. Without this important life skill, children will have much more difficulty dealing with others as they grow and mature. Punishment for these kinds of actions will be cumulative: If you grounded them from video games for a time period before, it is time to take the system away completely for a much longer time—permanently if necessary—until your children learns the respect that you require from them.

DIANE: *As a parent, saying, "You're grounded for two weeks," is a no-brainer way of ending the discussion, right? No…because in the end, you don't really know if two weeks is too long, too short, or just right. Sort of a Goldilocks problem! When we first started putting Chad or Scott on the couch as a time-out, we didn't have a "rule" knowing what* *to do. We knew he was little and couldn't sit still for long so we waited just until he was beginning to get antsy and then asked him what he did wrong, asked him to apologize, give us a hug, and go play. I guess it became instinctive for us to know that the less information you give the offender the more control you keep. Half the time we didn't know how long to "ground them" from their bikes or their Legos, so our plan of not telling them how long just developed on its own. It did seem to work very well for the Finkbeiner family. We also used that as a way of controlling our own anger or frustration, by taking us out of the equation sooner. We had much more control and empathy after a short break from the situation.*

3. Teaching responsibility may be more difficult if your child is older now. You have already established a working relationship with them whether you know it or not. The interactions that you have had as they were growing up have shaped their impression of what they can get away with. As you begin to change that relationship, your child will begin to resist that change; the more you push for change, the more they will push for a return to the

way things were. You have to be aware that this conflict is necessary for change to occur. How much "I hate you" are you willing to endure to ensure that your child's future will be brighter? It will take work, but isn't it worth it?

DIANE: *What if you have a 10-year-old who has been raised under different rules? How much harder will it be for you to become more decisive now? Immensely! Just imagine a 10-year-old girl named Jane who is accustomed to getting her own way most of the time. Do you think she will calmly fold and begin doing things your way? Of course not! She will fight you tooth and nail. She knows she can break you down…she's done it before. So you must stick to your guns. You might have to tell her "No" thirty times before she actually believes it. If you become lax even once, you revert to the beginning and start over where you now have to reaffirm your decisions—probably that thirty, multiplied by another ten. You have given Jane the knowledge that you won't stick to the new plan. But if you mean what you say about wanting a better life for her in the future, you can't give up on her. Don't be a wimp, find that control that you really want and* *use it.*

4. Children are very resilient. Because of this fact, it is important to change your punishments according to your child's individual range of acceptance. The most effective way to modify behavior is to find out what item your child values most and use that information to help you. If your child "can't live without" her phone, her phone should be the first thing you take away when she gets into trouble (even if it makes your life as a parent harder). If the behavior does not change, you MUST be WILLING to take away items permanently because, under all but the most extreme cases, it will not escalate to this point.

CHAD: *One of our favorite toys growing up was our Nintendo game system. My brother and I loved that piece of equipment more than almost anything, and because of this, it was a perfect pressure point for us. One time when we were fairly young we were playing Nintendo and were told by our dad to clean up the toys in front of the storage room in the basement so that he could get in there to do some work. We said that we would do it right away and he went back out to the garage to work on other things. We completely forgot about the chore we were supposed* *to complete. My dad came back in from the garage later expecting our chore to be complete since we were still playing games. Once Scott and I heard our names being called, (actually yelled), from the basement, we knew we were in big trouble. We ran downstairs and took a major tongue-lashing from our dad, who was very understandably upset. He told us to get to work cleaning and when we were done we went back up to finish our game, only to find our Nintendo system was missing...nothing left but the wires hanging from the TV. When we finally got up the courage to ask where it was, we were told, in no uncertain terms, that it was gone and if we asked about it again it would be thrown away permanently. Would my dad have really thrown away a perfectly good gaming system? Yes, I believe he would in order to teach us a valuable lesson. A few weeks later, it showed up in the den again, but only because we never brought up that it was gone, nor did we ask when it might be back.*

5. One of the hardest things to do as a parent or caring teacher is to stand by idly and watch your children fail. We are hard-wired as humans to help those we care for

to succeed; however, in today's society, this tendency has become a form of enabling. We no longer try to help our children succeed; we bail them out of learning situations and teach them that someone else will always be there to fix things. Unless you are willing to bail your children out of situations until they are 40 (and still living in your basement), you need to instill in them a sense of responsibility that will help guide them to a productive future.

> **DIANE:** *A mom has a son in college and is so proud of her young man. She is amazed at how much work he has to do, so being the good mom that she is, she begins to edit and then write his paper for him. SHE stays up late at night after receiving a "Help!" email from him on the eve of a deadline. She writes the paper and emails it back to him in the nick of time. That son no longer has a sense of independence or accomplishment that would encourage more responsibility for his future. This loving Mom's helpfulness has been a detriment to her son's growth.*

6. When was the last time you got in the car and drove to your child's school to drop off a "forgotten" lunch or permission slip? How about the last time you "helped"

your students with homework by completing the assignments for them? These gestures, although helpful in the short term, are very counterproductive in the long run for your child's future. As unfortunate as missing a field trip due to a forgotten permission slip is, it is a lesson that teaches responsibility better than most others. Once your child knows that it is his or her choice to remember or to forget, and more importantly, that you will not bail him out, his level of responsibility transfers from your hands to his—right where it should be.

CHAD: *When I was a kid I loved soccer. I played on lots of teams and played nearly every weekend of my life growing up. My parents would always ask me before we left the house, "Do you have everything?" My response was always "yup," even if I didn't know what was in my soccer bag and what was not. It did not happen often, but I do recall two separate times when the soccer socks that were put on my bed did not make it into my soccer bag before we left because I "forgot" to put them in. When I arrived at the game and started to get ready to play, I realized that my socks were missing. Now, my parents had enough time to run back home and grab my socks for me before the game started, and certainly before the second half started, but they refused. They were not mad at me; if anything they had a look of sympathy on their faces, but they told me that it was my responsibility and if I forgot them, then I guess I wouldn't be able to play that day. One of the games I was able to play with the help of a friend who had an extra pair of socks for me to borrow, while the other I sat on the sidelines watching my team for the whole game with tears in my eyes. I'm sure that was very hard for my parents to see, but they stuck with it knowing that it would make me more responsible in the future. It did, and I could not be more grateful.*

7. Learning about consequences from a young age is extremely important. Do you remember a time when you could get pulled over by the police for making a "mistake" of any kind and they would give you that "look," tell you that they never wanted to see you making that mistake ever again, and tell you to head straight home? Those days are gone. Your children NEED to know that the choices that they make will affect them more now than ever before in our nation's history. The consequences

for being "young and dumb" have become life-altering; preventing people from obtaining jobs, owning property, or obtaining a loan.

> **CHAD:** *Recently there was a story in the news that highlighted a young woman whose teaching job had been terminated due to a photograph posted on her Facebook page. It was a photograph taken of her when she was in college, drinking with friends. There was nothing else to the photo, but the school district had an enforced no-tolerance policy toward drinking, as it was a private school. Since then, companies all across the country have turned to "cyber stalking" as a way of digging up dirt on job applicants. A simple photo (taken years before she was ever in her career) cost this young woman her job. What consequences might your children have to deal with as they are growing up? In today's society of cell phone cameras, internet postings, and tabloid-style newscasting, your child cannot afford to make the same mistakes that earlier generations were able to make.*

8. The computer may be one of the greatest assets that our modern society has created, but for children, it can be

the most dangerous piece of equipment in any household. Most people know that children are naïve, but being teachers, we get a chance to see just how far that goes. Children see technology as exciting and interesting, but the danger of that technology is not a focus in their lives. If at all possible, the computer should be used in the same room as parents or other family in order to ensure that it is being used correctly and safely. If it is not possible to use the computer with the family (laptop), it is your obligation to "check in" on your children while they're using the computer. If they quickly hit a button when you walk in, you may want to go look over their shoulder to see how many windows they are "actually" looking at.

CHAD: *I had a girl in class a few years ago who turned in a project describing her life. One of the items on her project was a "YouTube" video that she and her friends made. They thought that it was a hilarious video, and when I asked them if they ever thought that it might make them prey for online predators, they said that they only posted the video under their first names, so they were safe. What they didn't understand was that they were putting themselves at risk anyway. In the video, the girls were lip-syncing* *to their favorite song, they were wearing sweatshirts clearly showing the school's name, and although she and her friends only posted the videos under their first names, they did have unique names. With these two pieces of information a predator would be able to figure out who these girls were and where they lived with very little effort. Fortunately for these girls, after I told them this information they chose to delete all of their "YouTube" posts.*

9. As we've said before, your kids will test the limits of your boundaries. At some point the testing turns into deceit or lying. I know what some of you are thinking: "My child doesn't lie to me!" You're right; your children probably don't lie to you on a regular basis, but believe me they will try lying to you even if they don't want to. In these instances, you need to let them know that you are aware that they are lying, and your most effective way to break them is to have a little fun with them. Make your child stick to his or her story instead of yelling at him right away. Making kids feel guilty is tenfold more effective than yelling. Give them a chance to come clean, and if they don't (they won't on the first try) give them another chance. If they still do not fold, start to play the

guilt card. Make them feel like you don't trust them and it will make everything that they try to do from that point forward more difficult for you to comply with.

CHAD: *When I was in junior high, our family had a dog named Corky-the absolute sweetest and the absolute dumbest dog you've ever seen. It was my job to let the dog out when I got home from school, but because Corky was...let's say intellectually challenged, taking her out to go to the bathroom was a huge process. One winter afternoon I chose not to let her out and decided to just wait until my Mom got home from school (she'd usually let the dog out when she got home so that Corky would not get "too excited" on the floor). I went outside to start shoveling the driveway as my Mom was pulling in. We said "hi" and talked briefly, then she went in to let the dog out. My Mom came back out and walked right up to me and asked if I had let the dog out when I got home. (I was one of those kids who didn't lie to my parents...ever) I said, "Yup" before I even knew I was lying. My Mom kinda cocked her head to the side and said, "Really, you did, huh?" Now I knew I was in trouble and I tried to stick with the* *lie. I said "Yeah, as soon as I got home." "Huh—that's interesting...'cause there's no footprints in the snow...are you sure?" "Yeah, I'm sure." This is the point where my Mom gave me "the look"--you know that look too, don't you?! My Mom turned around and didn't say another word, just marched toward the house shaking her head. That was all it took! I dropped the shovel and ran to her, half-yelling, "I lied, I didn't take her out—I don't even know why I said that! I'm sorry, I'm sorry, I don't even know why I lied!" To tell the honest truth, I don't even remember what happened after that because it's not the outcomes that your kids will remember; it's the lessons.*

10. As the previous story illustrates, it's not about the punishment, it's about the fear of the unknown. When children know that the punishment for any behavior will be predictable, they can weigh the positives against the known punishment. Your power as a parent or teacher comes in the form of mystery. As we have stated before, your children should be unaware of just how far you will take a punishment; they must BELIEVE that anything is possible.

DIANE: *So here's my side of the same story. I came home from school and there was my sweet Chad out shoveling the driveway. "What a great kid," I'm thinking. I headed into the house, down to the laundry room where Corky stayed when we were outside. I patted her on the head, but didn't speak to her because with excitement accidents can happen! I took her outside, noticed the lovely, fresh snow, and thought, "I wonder what the boy will say!?" After Corky did her thing, I went back outside to ask Chad "the question," not really expecting a lie. He really was an honest kid. But here came this big lie right out in front of us. My idea was to let him hang himself, and see just how far he would let this go. I could see some sort of a life lesson on the horizon. As I walked away from Chad, shaking my head, he came barreling at me, apologizing, almost sobbing. I remember telling him, "You know, the bad part isn't in the not taking the dog out. It's in the lying to me…I didn't think you could do that to me." It was all said in a very calm voice, and he could feel the disappointment in me. We hugged for a long time and went inside. I'm not sure what happened after that either-some discussion, some picking up dog* *poop. Regardless, our relationship was strengthened as a result of slow, calm talking, not angry shouting.*

11. Once you truly believe that your job is to provide for, protect, and guide your kids, you should not need to be liked by your kids every second of every day. What you are searching for is your child's love, not your child's friendship. Part of your job as a parent or teacher is to make your child's life easier, and if allowing them to place the blame on you in order to save face with their peers will make their lives easier, you should be okay with this idea. Children need an escape, and you are that escape, as long as it is not overused, especially in lieu of responsibility.

CHAD: *When I was in high school, I was friends with many of the sports heroes from our school, and was always invited to the after parties on Friday nights following the football game. I knew that it was not my scene, with all of the drinking and partying, but I didn't want my friends to think that I was "uncool." Fortunately for me, my parents allowed me to place the blame on them in order to make the decisions that I knew in the back of my mind were right. I would usually tell anyone who asked me to join them for a party that my parents wouldn't let* *me go to any party after a football game no matter whose house it was at. The truth was I never even asked them because I didn't really want to go myself, but I wanted to save face with my friends. I used this "out" quite often while growing up in order to make the right choices.*

12. If there is only one thing that you take away from this system, this is it! "Game face and personal space" is the key to our success as teachers and your key to success with your child. Most parents react to children the way they would react to other adults. When cornered or angry, we yell. In one of life's biggest ironies, children do not respond well to yelling. What they do respond well to though is intimidation. You, as a parent or teacher, need to master your own unique game face. It's a look that says you are serious and "playtime is over." To maximize the usefulness of this face you must get right up next to your child, as well as getting down to eye level. There will be no yelling; in fact, the quieter you talk, the more you throw them off. Your power lies with their inability to read what you are thinking. They will, however, be able to read your body language and your…that's right, your game face! Now your game face does not involve anger or clenched teeth.

In order to be the one in total control of the situation, you must possess a sense of calm throughout all that you do with your children.

MYTH 3

POUTING, WHINING AND CRYING ALWAYS WORKS

As babies, before we learn to talk, we whine and cry to get what we need to survive. Unlike most of our other toddler tendencies, this one seems to stick around a while longer. A young child may begin to cry and whine or pout when not getting what he or she wants, but think about it—isn't this how he learned to be fed, to be changed, to be hugged, and even to be loved? It is a very hard trend to break. As we have already stated, learned behavior can become hardwired, which means that it will take a lot of willpower, planning, and patience to change this behavior. The way that these behaviors were learned was through a process of positive reinforcement, and, unfortunately for today's parents and teachers, it will only be changed through the same process—positive reinforcement. Here is what we believe will help bring this process to you and your family:

1. NO still means NO.

2. There is a difference between crying softly from disappointment and crying to obtain something.

3. Light-hearted playful actions and words are extremely effective.

4. Never give in to whining, - even if it's what you want also.

5. Do not make excuses for your child to misbehave.

6. React to their actions, not their overall character.

7. Newton's law of parenting

8. Crying due to pain or heartache should never be punished

9. Always take care of the problem IN the moment.

10. Never underestimate your action's impact on their value system.

1. Oh, look, it's our friend "no means no" again. Now we know you're getting tired of this one, but it really is the key to your success with this program. Firm but fair will save your sanity. And now we can finally put this one to rest…..maybe!

2. There are basically only three responses that a child can give to any situation in which you have just said "no" and each one should be handled differently. The first kind of response is called "internalized acceptance." When a child knows that you are in charge and that your answer is final, he begins to understand that no matter what he does, the scenario will not change. Internalized acceptance can be seen in a child who, although disappointed, does not cry or make a scene to try to change the outcome. This child will look somewhat let down but will not make faces of disgust, anger, or defiance. In this case, you have done your job well and your child deserves praise when you reach the car or outdoors.

The second kind of response is called "advanced disappointment." This type of response is usually seen when a child is extremely excited about something and then receives a "no." It is marked by gentle tears, and/or some pouting. Advanced disappointment is an acceptable response as long as it does not escalate to anything even approaching a tantrum. When children exhibit this type of response, a discussion about how to act in public and why we can't always get everything we want is the appropriate path. Many times just the explanation to them of what you were thinking will be enough to make you feel a little better and to get them to know that you still love them enough to let them know what you are thinking and why.

The third and final response is called...that's right; a "temper tantrum." This is an unacceptable response and leads to punishment. Tantrums, however, are the only response that have a "negative reinforcement" consequence. Making a scene in public is something that is not tolerated by society and therefore should not be tolerated by you as a parent or teacher. In no case should you give in to their disappointment once you have said "no;" it will be hard and it will hurt your heart, but it is what is best for them and deep down you'll know you're right.

CHAD: *One of my most vivid memories of knowing what to say even though I was livid and clearly upset has to do with a snowmobile trip that I was invited to go on with my friends. My parents knew the parents of this friend of mine, but not well enough* *to totally guarantee my absolute safety while in their care. When I asked (all excited and bouncy) if I could go on the snowmobile trip, my Mom told me "no." I was crushed; I wanted to go so badly, and couldn't understand why in the world she would say no. I almost threw a temper tantrum but knew that wouldn't change the outcome and decided to play Mom's game hoping to talk her into it. I said, "Okay, but can I at least ask why?" Mom said to me that she didn't like the idea of me riding a snowmobile without her or my dad around and that she loved me too much to let me go. That is a very hard concept to argue with: "I wish you didn't love me so much then." "I'm sorry but I do." There really isn't any winning of that argument from the child's perspective, and so I didn't go on the snowmobile trip. However, I did walk away from the conversation still really upset, but with the absolute knowledge that I was loved. I forgot all about it by the weekend when we went sledding as a family.*

3. One of the most important concepts that we support is the ability to use kindness, love, and playfulness to change behavior. Most parents and teachers attempt to

change behavior by yelling or punishing when a little playful humor would probably get the job done without the resentment that follows after being punished. Letting the child know that they are walking a fine line between playfulness and punishment with a look or a gesture is a non-threatening way to get your point across while also allowing you time to think about what the consequence might be if the behavior continues.

DIANE: *I'm sure you have seen a parent/child interaction in which the child is sad or upset and the parent says, "Oh, honey, what's wrong? Are you okay?" The first thing that does is encourage the behavior. Obviously, something must be wrong if Mom doesn't know if I'm okay. In our home, when that sad or upset moment began and the lower lip began to tremble, we would smile and teasingly say, "Uh, oh, I'm gonna step on your lip—watch out!" We would come toward the kids with smiling eyes and grabbing fingertips, and almost always a giggle would erupt. Then, we could laugh and hug and move on to a new activity. The same idea works with injuries. No matter how upset you are about an injury, especially one involving blood, you must* *control your emotions to benefit your child. Calm, strong hugs, words of encouragement like, "You'll be fine, it's okay, let's take care of you," and positive forward action will give your child the ability to undo the rising panic and trust that you will "make it all better."*

4. All right, I know we said that we were done with the "no meaning no" thing but you didn't really believe that did you? Well, I guess we're going to have to rephrase it just a little. Here we go: Never give in to whining, even if it's what you want also. As parents or teachers there are times where we have to put what we actually want aside because it is better and more productive to take that time to teach our children a valuable lesson.

DIANE: *When the boys were kids we ate at home as a family every night. While I was cooking dinner, the boys were finishing their homework and my husband was either getting home from work or working on hobbies in the garage. Our boys were both in sports and sometimes it was very difficult to find the energy to cook dinner at home after a game or practice. Once in a while we would stop on the way home at a fast food restaurant.*

The boys LOVED it because it was not a regular occurrence, but every now and then they would make the mistake of asking if we were going to get McDonald's and I would say "maybe" to give myself time to think of the situation and whether or not we really could get fast food that night. Before I could answer yes, one or both of them had started to whine about how it's not fair that we don't get to eat out more often. Even though I had decided that we were going to get McDonald's and that it was the best idea of the day, I would turn to them and give that all important "game face." Unfortunately for all of us, sometimes that was not quite enough and the whining continued. I truly did want to eat fast food that night and I truly did NOT want to go home and cook, but in order to teach my boys that they were never going to get their way with bad behavior, that is exactly what I did; I went home and cooked. It was more important to me that I followed through with what I said than to make my own life easier for that one day.

5. It's interesting being a teacher because you get to see a lot of behavior origin during parent-teacher conferences.

You would be amazed how often a child's poor behavior mirrors the behavior of the parents or guardians in the household. One of the most prevalent examples is how often parents make excuses for their child's bad behavior. Sometimes it is as seemingly insignificant as saying, "Oh, he didn't mean it," when your child tells you "No," but it leads to you saying the same thing when he is telling you to shut up and leave him alone: "Oh, he didn't mean it." Behaviors, much like learning, build upon themselves; it's the theory of escalation. Before you know it you're in the midst of a nuclear war with your child and have no way of regaining control. Giving your children an excuse of any kind is a form of crippling. Unless they learn how to function on their own without you and your unconditional excuses they are bound to fail, and will require your assistance for everything that they do.

DIANE: *I met a parent from school at a local craft fair who had her fourth grade son with her. As she and I began to talk, he started pushing her in the back forcefully! He continued shoving her, knocking her off balance, and trying to gain her attention. She was a bit embarrassed, but not much, as she said to me, "Oh, he's just in a hurry to leave." I don't believe* *the young man learned anything appropriate that day. He did learn that interrupting was fine and that he could, literally, push his mother around without consequences of any kind. A better response from his mom would have been for her to say, "Excuse me," to me and turn around for some important face time with her son. Without this all-important talk her son will never learn what is acceptable in society, let alone what is acceptable in the family.*

6. As teachers, we are constantly challenged to separate behavior from character. More often than not, children know when they are doing something wrong and are usually not surprised when a punishment comes their way. When we punish an action, we are saying to the child that "what they did" was wrong and that we believe that it was simply a mistake to learn from for the future. However, when we punish a child because he or she is "always getting in trouble," we are saying to that child that "who they are" is wrong. We begin to make them think that they are always going to screw up, and this is just another time that we are disappointed in who they are on a personal level. When you can get a child to believe that you are on his side and only want what is best for him, you can earn

trust and respect even while punishing. The key to this is to ACTUALLY believe in your child. You must find a way to separate the punishing from the person and let your child know that you do not "want" to punish him, but that it is what's best to prepare him for the future. A great way to illustrate this to him is to have fun with learning the boundaries. Just because it's called a punishment does not mean that you can't have fun with it.

CHAD: *The first day of class every year, I go through a list of "rules" that I enforce in my classroom. Respect, Integrity, Work Ethic, and Honor are the most important, but I also have a fun rule that helps to lighten the atmosphere in the classroom. This is called my "garbage rule." I tell my students that one of my pet peeves is students shooting balled-up paper toward the garbage can. I dislike this because if they miss, most often they do not pick it up, they simply leave it there for someone else to clean up. The garbage rule states that anyone in my classroom (including myself) who shoots a piece of paper and misses must then go pick it up off the floor with their teeth. I then model the behavior by throwing paper on the floor and picking it up in the recommended* *manner. As you can imagine, many of the students squirm and laugh and get the most disgusted faces. At this point I tell them that if they wish not to pick up paper with their teeth, the solution is simple: place your garbage in the can instead of shooting. It is a rule that is fondly remembered as the students often come back and tell me how much they miss my class—especially the garbage rule! It's fun for all but does not punish those who follow the rule of placing the garbage in its proper place. This fun rule helps them to see that I have boundaries, but it does not mean that we can't have fun while learning those boundaries.*

7. Newton's Law of parenting states that "every action has an equal and opposite reaction." Okay, so that's just his third law of motion; however, it can be adapted to parenting and teaching. Knowing that there will always be consequences for your actions is an important lesson to learn early in life. If you happen to be speeding down the road and a police officer sees you, what happens? You get a ticket. And when you decide not to show up to work for a few weeks...yup, that's right, you get fired. This is why you, as a parent, want to focus on correcting actions while

it's still possible to effect permanent change. The severity of any punishment should therefore be in direct relation to the severity of the action. How far should you go with that severity? Should you go as far as a swat on the butt? Unfortunately, we can't give you the answer for this one; it has to be a decision that you (and your spouse) come to on your own.

DIANE: *Our family philosophy for behavior was to ALWAYS respond to inappropriate behavior, but we were never very pleased to handle repeat offenses. One day we were at Grandma and Grandpa's house for dinner. Chad and Scott asked if they could go outside to kick the soccer ball. We said, "Sure, but be careful." Clearly, the instructions were too vague as two minutes later we heard a "Wham!" as the soccer ball hit the siding on the house. Dad headed out and said, "Guys, knock it off; quit hitting Grandpa's house." The boys answered, "Okay, sorry!" Not even two seconds later "Wham!" and again the ball smacked the house. This time Dad headed out, gave each boy a quick smack on the rear, took the ball, and scooted them back inside. Overkill? Maybe for some, but for us emphasizing respect for others'* *property as well as listening to our directions was paramount.*

8. Now we come to the touchy part of punishment versus rewards, especially when working with a topic like crying. Crying due to pain or heartache should "never" be punished. There is a reason that people cry; it is a physical mechanism that helps to alleviate mental and/or physical pain. Because it is such an important part of our humanity, it is also equally important not to snuff that emotional fire out. Now, what is it they say about "never saying never?" Oh, that's right—don't do it! There should always be room for crying to help deal with a physical or mental pain; however, you, as a parent or teacher, need to make sure that it is true pain and that the tears are not being used to obtain something, even if that something is only attention. Many children will learn from an early age that crying will get them attention. This knowledge is then adapted to other situations. When a child begins to use situations in which they could be upset to get attention or to manipulate people, it becomes another crutch for them to fall back on instead of being responsible for themselves and their obligations. A loss of someone close or a physical injury is a perfectly acceptable time to cry,

or even whine a bit. Of the two, emotional pain is much more challenging to spot, but is no less important, and needs to be consoled, not punished.

> **DIANE:** *The emotion of sadness is an important and necessary one. We all sometimes need the relief of tears. Kids can grow up learning that tears are an individual expression of sadness or that they are a mechanism for interaction and attention from adults. I'm sure you've seen the children in the toy store howling, usually without tears, because they're not getting what they want. It may even escalate into a tantrum. This is definitely a show for attention and deserves some consequences. There were times when Chad and Scott would be in a toy store or a grocery store and wanted something that we wouldn't agree to. They might look sad, even show a few silent tears—no punishment there. They were allowed to show that emotion of sadness, but it didn't last; it was sadness of the moment and then we moved on.*

9. Always taking care of the problem "in the moment" seems to be a huge obstacle in the world in which we

live. Parents and teachers have become afraid of what others will think or do if a punishment is given in public. There is that all-too-familiar feeling of everyone staring at you, wondering what you are going to do when your child is acting up. What many people have resorted to is the classic "You just wait 'til we get home…You're gonna get it!" The problem with this course of action is twofold. First, let's face it; by the time you get home, punishment is the last thing on your mind. In fact, to be brutally honest, you probably don't really remember just how upset or embarrassed you were. Second, your child is much like a puppy; if there is too much time between the action and the punishment, the correlation between the two is lost.

CHAD: *Being a teacher, I know that it is hard to punish "in the moment." When I have a student who is acting up in class, it can be difficult to reprimand him when so much work needs to get done in each class period, but I believe that what I am teaching about character is so much more beneficial to all students in the classroom that I am willing to put lesson plans on hold for a few minutes. Most often if someone is out of line in my class, I give a visual warning (the game face) followed by a verbal* *warning ("I'm not going to tell you again" or "last chance").*

If the behavior continues I will stop class and take the student to the hall to have a one-on-one chat. This conversation is usually me getting right up in his or her face and speaking very quietly but VERY firmly about what I expect to happen if I allow the student back in my classroom. The other students do not know what I'm saying, but they do know that I have hit my limit with disrespect and will not tolerate any more that day. Taking time to talk to one student, in turn, corrects the behavior of the whole class. The last thing I say to the reprimanded student before we return to class is, "This conversation was between you and me—no one else needs to hear the details while we're in class...got it?" This is to keep the whispering of "what happened" or "what did he say to you" to a minimum.

10. Modeling the behavior that you wish to see in your child is essential. The old phrase used to be "do as I say, not as I do,"...I know, I know, you hated hearing that too, didn't you? The reason we hated hearing that was because it emphasized that we (as the child) had absolutely no

control, and that what we were being told to do did not really apply once we reached adulthood. Everything that we hope to see our children become, we must strive to be now. The more you model the behaviors that you want to see, the easier it will be for your children to show them to you, because it will be a mutual endeavor. You need to make sure that your children know beyond a shadow of a doubt that they are your first priority and that you are willing to do anything to help them succeed.

DIANE: *I was at school one cold, snowy January day. It had been snowing a lot recently so there were mounds of snow piled along the sides of the road made by the snowplows. We have no sidewalks in the subdivision so all the kids wear down a path in the snow-covered grass. There is much traffic from parents and school buses picking up children from school. As I left one day on my way to a workshop, most of the traffic and children had passed the first turn that I took. I saw a mom and child on the path, the mom in front and the seven-year-old daughter following in her snowy tracks. Sounds okay so far, right? Except that the mother was on her cell phone with her daughter about 15 feet behind her. So many* *things could have gone wrong: the daughter could have slipped into the traffic, hurt herself, or worse. None of those things happened, but the daughter learned that Mom's conversations on the phone were more important than learning what had happened to her at school that day. If you were a part of very many days like that, would you wonder why your response might be, "Nothing," when finally asked, "What happened at school today?" Kids believe your actions more than your words.*

MYTH 4

MANNERS ARE FOR GEEKS

Chivalry, couth, manners; it doesn't matter what you call it; the concept is one of the most important skills that a person can possess in his lifetime. With this skill and little else a person can make a life for him or herself. Manners have a way of changing the way society views a person. When was the last time someone said, "Thank you" to you? Do you even remember? Did you reply with, "You're welcome" or were you too busy or caught up in your own life? What did that just teach your children? What makes manners so great is that they are an internal mechanism that needs no prompting or recognition in order to be used; however, the impact that they can make can change the course of a life.

1. Social graces improve society's impression of you - whether valid or not.

2. If you have REAL manners it becomes hard to be disrespectful.

3. Start young if possible, with "Please and thank you."

4. Start NOW if they are no longer young; it's one of the easiest things to change in a child's behavior.

5. How to encourage the use of manners:
   a. Use them yourself.
   b. Always reinforce the good.
   c. Always correct the bad…not necessarily punish; but correct.

6. Be playful in your corrections!

7. Chivalry is not dead…nor should it ever disappear.

8. A good handshake is mandatory for both boys and girls.

9. Real apologies versus fake or forced apologies.

10. Appropriate language choices.

1. The ability to make the general population have a positive view of you upon first impression is an incredibly helpful tool to possess. We're not talking about having to make society like you; instead, just being you and allowing society to be impressed by you is tenfold better. When we look at people, we automatically make assumptions about them based on dress, physical features, speech, etc. This is not inherently bad; it's just human nature. However, it can be manipulated. One of the easiest ways to manipulate people's impressions of you is through your first impression behavior.

CHAD: *When I went back to school to obtain my teaching degree, I went to a college where manners seemed to be lacking in most of my classes. On the first day of class for one of my education courses, I walked into the room and noticed a good-looking girl sitting up front so I decided to sit next to her and strike up a conversation. She was a very pleasant girl not unlike many I had met before, but I didn't take much more notice than that. The professor came by to hand out a pop quiz to see what we knew. When he mentioned the term "pop quiz" most of the class groaned, but when he came to our row and handed* the tests to this same girl, she said, "Thank you." It was such a simple gesture, but because it had been so long since I had heard someone thank a teacher for giving them anything (let alone a quiz) my ears instantly perked up. I immediately saw this girl in a whole new light. Her manners had given me an instant impression about her personality. She became one of my close friends over the years, but if not for that first impression of kindness and respect, I may not have even taken the time to get to know her.

When we, as teachers, see someone who thanks us for passing out a test, we instantly have a positive impression of not only that student but the parents who raised that student. This is not a failsafe test of a person's overall character by any means. We all remember the guy in high school who was a total creep but was always respectful and courteous to the parents of the girl he was interested in, right?! How was he so successful in conning the parents into believing he was a great guy? He did it through the effective use of manners. Manners will take you everywhere in this life but only when they are real *and truthful.*

2. You can get further in life with manners than perhaps with any other skill. So how do we develop people with true manners and not just a bunch of high school creeps with some manipulation skills? The answer is parenting. It is up to parents and teachers to cultivate manners in children from the time they are young, and they must continue to cultivate those manners throughout the child's lifetime. Once the manners are ingrained and have become part of who you are, it becomes very difficult to be that creep. When you are used to holding doors open for people, saying thank you, and telling the truth, doing anything that falls outside of this feels uncomfortable. If having a child who is respectful, honest, and all-around good is important to you, the use of manners is your key.

DIANE: *When I was teaching sixth grade, I read a small article in the newspaper about a mayor in a New England city who had come up with a Courtesy Campaign for people in his town. I loved the idea since our town had had a lot of rude confrontations among the people and the leaders at township meetings. I talked to my class about the article and asked what they thought. Since we'd* *been working on kindness and manners for months, they decided they'd like to try something like a Courtesy Campaign for our area. We began making posters and flyers encouraging more civil behaviors, such as being kind to everyone, smiling more, using manners and kindness. They all designed their own flyers, colored them, and decided where they should go: offices, stores, government buildings. They then decided to mail some to businesses asking if they would be interested in purchasing any for their own use. The class was so excited when responses came in actually requesting more posters. This endeavor only lasted about a month, but the kids knew they were spreading a great message and understood that every little bit can make a difference.*

3. Getting a young child to use manners is not only fun and easy but rewarding for everyone involved. Remember our friend Pavlov? He may have preferred dogs, but that positive reinforcement lesson lives on. Young children will repeat actions that have brought about a positive reaction in adults. So before you hand them the toy or blanket that they asked for or the ring that they want to look at, make them say, "Please." Besides, if you start young enough,

it even sounds cute…"Peez"! Have your children say, "Please" and "Thank you" for EVERYTHING; not just the things that they want to receive. A good rule of thumb is anytime someone hands them anything it should be accompanied by a, "Thank you." With young children, you may have to ask for the response as a reminder until it becomes second nature to the child.

DIANE: *Every Halloween when Chad and Scott were little their dad and I would take turns taking them trick-or-treating. One would stay home passing out treats while the other walked with the boys. After an hour, we would switch places. We would start close to home because the neighbors were encouraging and complimented the boys' costumes so they felt comfortable. Sometimes they got a little too comfortable and needed to be reminded of what to do when someone gives you something. A nudge and, "What do you say?" was all it took. Usually one reminder was enough. Even today as I pass out candy at my home, I'm impressed by good manners. If teenagers don't say "Thank you" it's very discouraging, but when little ones don't, it's just sad because they haven't been taught manners.*

This year I had a dad come up the steps to the door, leaving his two-year-old sitting in a wagon with his four-year-old brother standing at the bottom of the steps. Dad took two pieces of candy for them and promptly left. No "hi," no conversation about his two little cuties, no thank you at all. I wanted to yell at his retreating back, "You're welcome!!" but I didn't. I figured it wouldn't do any good.

4. Getting older children to use manners is usually not as cute; however, it does not have to be unpleasant for either you or your child. To get older children to say, "Please" or "Thank you" most often requires the same persistence that teaching young children does, only once the older child understands the concept, the number of times that you have to verbally remind him drops significantly. At that point "the look" is all that is required.

CHAD: *In my classroom, I cannot tell you how many times I hear Johnny yell to his friend from across the room, "Jenny, get me a piece of paper while you're up there!" At this point, I always look at Johnny and give him my raised eyebrow look that says, "Aren't you forgetting something?" Johnny will look at me and say, "What?!", and at this point, I will call out* *to Jenny while still looking at Johnny, "Jenny, don't even think about getting Johnny a piece of paper unless he is respectful to you." Johnny will smile and call out, "Jenny can you PLEASE get me a piece of paper?" I smile, Johnny smiles, and Jenny smiles; the entire class understands what I am doing, and no one else asks for paper for the rest of that hour without saying, "Please" or "Thank you."*

5. One of the most important parts of rearing children that is often overlooked is how much adult action accounts for child action. Parents and teachers must always be aware of what they are doing and must model the behavior that they are trying to encourage. Parents should use manners as often as possible if they wish to bring that trait out in their children. In our hectic and time-crunched world, it seems hard to remember to thank people or take the extra two seconds to hold a door open for the person behind you. Just because your life, as an adult, has more constraints on your time does not mean that it's okay to model behavior contrary to what you are trying to teach. When your children then model proper behavior, let them know that you saw it and are proud of them. When they slip and neglect to model appropriate behavior, correct it

with playful humor so it does not seem like a chore, but more of a family game that is always being played.

DIANE: *A teacher at our school has a little boy about eighteen months old. She brought him to school one day, and, of course, everyone was watching the little guy. All of a sudden he sneezed and said, "'Cuze me!" Everyone laughed and told him what a good boy he was. Mom was proud; son was happy...it was a great reinforcing moment for good behavior and manners being taught at a very early age.*

6. Being playful in your corrections seems like an oxymoron, but in reality it makes perfect sense. What we are trying to do as parents or teachers is teach life lessons that will help guide our children through life in the most positive manner. And as we have stated earlier, yelling and anger accomplish much less than positive reinforcement. If you are at work and your boss starts yelling at you, are you likely to respond with eagerness to please or defiance in the face of authority? Most people are wired to respond better to positive forces, so use this to your advantage—make it fun for you and for your children to learn the lessons that will stick with them for the duration of their lives.

CHAD: *When I graduated from college, I made my way to the mountains to work as a ski instructor. The company I worked for had a written policy of lightheartedness at the workplace. They had all new employees watch a motivational video about "Pike Place Fish Market" in Seattle. In case you don't know, Pike Place became world famous for the interactions between its staff and customers. The Fishmongers literally throw fish to each other while putting on a show, even allowing the customers to join in. We watched this video and were told that the company wanted us to emulate this environment. There was only one problem: any time any of the employees would begin having fun with the guests and entertaining the crowd, they were moved to another station and reprimanded for "goofing off." The bottom line is that even in your household you need to have a vision of what you want and the rules you set forth for your children need to coincide with your overall goal. Have fun with your kids, enjoy their innocence, but let them know that you are still in charge without the negativity that so often accompanies "punishment."*

7. Chivalry is a term rarely heard in modern society, and also a term most often associated with men. However, the concept of helping others, being gracious, and possessing a sense of honor, is universal. When was the last time someone held a door open for you, or let you take the first taxi to pull up at the airport? Did you thank him or her? Would your child have done the same? One more question: "Where would they learn that they should have?" Chivalry is a skill that takes time to develop; humans are instinctively self-driven, and to create the will to help others first takes teaching from those we trust most. Yup, that's right, it comes down to you again—parents.

DIANE: *One of the things Chad and Scott loved to do from the time they were little was to hold doors open for others. It may have started with a slight nudge from us, but it quickly became a brotherly competition to see who could get there first to hold the door. It was always great when there were two doors so they could each hold one. Here again, we have positive feedback from adults: big smiles and thank you's. Don't you, even now, enjoy when another person shows a kindness such as holding a door for you? Doesn't it make you have a more* *positive opinion about that person? Simple manners, huge rewards!*

8. In a country where meeting someone for the first time or seeing someone after even a short absence is accompanied by a handshake, it is mandatory that our children learn the importance of a good, firm handshake. A proper handshake should be firm but not cause pain; it should move in a slight up and down motion but should not jar the other person's arm; and it should ALWAYS be accompanied by a look in the eyes. This again is one of those skills that must be learned through positive reinforcement—any time your child shakes your hand you should praise or correct. Finally, there is nothing wrong with practicing any or all of the skills that have been discussed, so practice them with your kids often. Again, make it your own personal family game.

DIANE: *When Chad was about two years old, his dad decided Chad needed to know how to shake hands correctly. He would stick out his hand until Chad grabbed on to it, and then shake it to show him how it is done. Chad grew into knowing the correct way by grabbing his dad's hand often. When friends would come over, Dad would tell Chad to shake* *hands and watch the adult's reaction. Chad loved the positive attention. When Scott came along, he learned not only from Dad but also from Chad. Once the boys knew they were expected to give and receive handshakes all the time, they began to watch the faces of the people they were greeting and gain insight into the "correctness" of the handshake. Each of the boys came home at one time or another feeling proud because Mr. So-and-So had congratulated them on a great handshake.*

9. Another one of the classic signs that show us as teachers that manners are falling by the wayside is the prevalence of the fake apology. Children today have a knack of knowing when to apologize so as not to get in trouble, but if you ask them why they are apologizing they have no idea why or what they have done wrong. This goes back to the earlier point about people instinctively being self-centered. Children, especially young children, need to understand that they cannot do whatever they want without having consequences, and when those consequences hurt someone else it MUST be followed by a true, heartfelt apology. Just one of the ways to make sure that the apology is true is to make your children state

what they are sorry for and not simply say "I'm sorry." "I'm really sorry that I broke your toy; I didn't mean to," is a much better indicator that your child knows that what he or she did was wrong and that the child is truly remorseful. Sometimes it's just good manners to apologize for being disruptive to other people.

> **CHAD:** *When Scott and I were very young, we were expected to be on our best behavior whenever we were out with our parents at a restaurant. We were not robots by any means, though; we had a great time playing games within our booths. Our favorite place to eat was Pizza Hut and it was always a treat when we went. Pizza Hut was fun for us in part because they gave you the straw for your beverage still wrapped. This meant that you could rip the end open and shoot the straw wrappers at each other like mini-blowguns. Occasionally, especially when we were very young, one of the straw wrappers would fly past our intended target and onto the table of another family. My parents were adamant that we had to go over to that table and apologize for interrupting their meal. It was scary as a child to go up to strangers and apologize for doing something*

wrong, but it did teach us how important it is to make amends for wrongdoings. Usually the families were so impressed by our behavior that any amount of animosity they may have harbored earlier disappeared; more often than not they smiled at us while telling us that it was not a problem at all.

10. The prevalence of foul language in childhood today is staggering. Foul language is not only profanity, but negative comments made toward other classmates including verbal bullying. Now you may be thinking, "That's not my child" and you're probably right, but are you sure? Are you absolutely 100 percent sure?! Think back to your childhood…was there anyone you ever made fun of, did you ever curse at anyone even though your parents told you that swearing was wrong? Why would your kids be any different in the world we live in today? We can even look at this a different way: do you swear at work or around your boss as much as you do when in your social circle? Unfortunately for your kids, their social circle IS at school. Kids today see more violence and hear more profanity than any previous generation. Their music, the internet, even television allows more to be shown than at any time before. This is why it is so much more important

today to teach those values, manners, and choices that you wish for your children to exemplify. Your language choice at work and at home is just that: a choice. Possibly more than any other behavior, it must be modeled for your children. Foul language and bad-mouthing of anyone WILL transfer to your children, whether you want it to or not.

> **DIANE:** *When Chad and Scott had company over, all house rules applied. We really never had problems with poor language from our boys because early "looks" kept them under control. But early on some of their friends would let slip with some word that was not acceptable, and we would say, "Oops! Give me five!!" with a smile. Yup! Push-ups!!*
>
> *The kids didn't mind them (great exercise, right?), we weren't angry, and the consequences were over with quickly. It seems pretty ridiculous, but maybe because it is ridiculous, it works.*
>
> *When everyone was home from college, a bunch of kids were in the house when a girl let loose with a "word." We didn't even have to say anything...the other kids said," Uh-oh—push-ups!!" Everyone was*

laughing, she looked at me, and I just shrugged my shoulders with a grin on my face. Did she do them? Of course, she did. Did she swear again at our house? Nope!

MYTH 5

I AM THE KING OF THE CASTLE

"Entitlement" is a word that didn't mean a whole lot in previous generations; it was thought that you earned what you received through hard work and dedication. Not so in this generation. Today's youth possess a sense of entitlement that is staggering. They honestly feel that they deserve things without having to work for them. This idea is either fostered or stifled early on in life. Does your child believe that the room in your house where they sleep is actually "their room?" That particular room may contain everything that your child believes to be his, but how did he get those possessions? It was because you allowed it. Therefore, all possessions in your "kingdom" are yours and not your children's. There must only be one king of the castle, and it must be you.

1. King by heredity – title must be earned.

2. Being given everything leads to a lack of appreciation and increase of expectation.

3. No such thing as "mine" when concerning child's property.

4. Doors WILL NOT be locked unless done so by the parents.

5. No permission is needed to enter a child's room—ever.

6. MONITOR computer use often—position in common room, if possible.

7. The only rights children have in the home are those that parents give to them.

8. Nothing you're doing "in the moment" is more important than your child's future.

1. The attitude that "I Am the King of the Castle" is a very dangerous attitude for a children to have because what they are really saying is that, "I have the power in this household." If your children truly believe that they are in control of what happens in the house, you will never get them to see your point of view or reasoning for any decision you make. The reason that parents hold the power is to set guidelines and boundaries for their children; owning the power to set the rules must be earned. In case you're wondering, it's earned through a lifetime of experiences that NEVER trump the experiences of the parent.

CHAD: *When Scott and I were little, we shared a bedroom. Unlike many children today, though, we knew that our room was not necessarily "ours." One of our favorite things to do was to make forts out of bed sheets that were tucked into our dresser drawers. We would then "camp out" for a couple of days. Even though these forts were in "our" room, we never created them without permission from our parents. WE knew that we HAD to get permission because if we tried to make the forts without getting permission, we would not be allowed to make them again for much, much longer (if ever). We never* *believed that our room was truly ours, but we never felt a lack of privacy or ownership growing up. It was this very beneficial coordination between parent and child that allowed us to work so well together throughout our growing up.*

2. One of the major problems with a sense of entitlement is that it is almost always accompanied by a lack of appreciation. If you never have to work for any of your possessions, you don't know what it feels like to have earned them. That sense of appreciation when you finally get what you have longed for, or when you can finally afford it after hard work, is priceless. It's that feeling that makes most of us work hard in the first place. What we really long for are not the possessions but the feeling of accomplishment that goes with them. Giving unconditionally to your kids should be reserved for love only...everything else they should have to work for.

CHAD: *When I was living in Colorado, I bought my first motorcycle. It was a family rule that we couldn't own a motorcycle until we moved out and were living on our own. The week I moved to Breckenridge, I began looking for "the perfect bike." I found the bike I had been dreaming about* *in the paper and called the guy up, made an offer, and four days later I was the proud owner of a new motorcycle. I had been dreaming of owning this very bike for years and now that I finally owned it, I vowed to keep it immaculate. I went so far as to take soap and brushes out during rain storms and wash it in the rain. I had that bike for just shy of ten years, and I never took it for granted because it was something that I had to work and wait for before I could get it. This metaphor is true for any object that your kids are longing to make theirs.*

3. For centuries, kids have been using the term "mine," so it should come as no surprise that they are still using the term today; however, what should come as somewhat of a surprise is that parents no longer tell their children that this is false. Anything that children consider theirs most likely came from you, in which case it would be yours. Even if the child bought the item with his or her "own money," where did that money come from: allowance, babysitting, even a job. Unless they are willing to pay part of the mortgage and help with the groceries, it is because of your generosity that they are able to purchase anything at all. Once your children believe that everything they

have is thanks to you, it is much harder for them to argue or question the decisions you make. In this kingdom, the king is a benevolent king…just don't try to take his throne or it's the dungeon for you. Creating a dungeon for your child is easy: just find the room in the house that has the least to do in it - that's your dungeon.

> **DIANE:** *Chad and Scott were never sent to their room as punishment—not alone and not together. They would always have been able to find something entertaining to do in there, and I wouldn't have been able to keep my eye on them. Instead they were sent to the couch in the living room where all they could do was look out the window and think. Yes, thinking was a big part of punishment because before they could leave they had to tell me why they had been there and apologize.*

4. We hear all too often about the child who got into an argument with the parent and wound up running up to his or her "room" and slamming the door shut. This is not only extremely disrespectful but completely unacceptable. That door belongs to you as the parent and King of the Household. Its slamming shut represents defiance and immaturity. The bedroom door of the child

is NEVER to be locked unless done so by the parents; this is non-negotiable. How, you ask, can you keep them from slamming the door or locking you out? Simple…take the door away. The next time your child slams that door, you come in with a screwdriver and pop the hinge pins out and take the door away completely. Once they learn to respect the family household, your household, they will have another try with a room which has a door to be shut calmly or not at all. Does this mean that children should have no say in their rooms? Absolutely not. What it means is that you, as a parent, must always have the final say in what goes on in your household. Once that respect level is obtained, you can then begin to give your children some room to express themselves.

CHAD: *When I was born, my dad painted my room to be the calming space a little boy would like. There was a rainbow painted on one wall with stickers of blue birds, a giant bunny, and Mickey Mouse. As my brother and I got older, our parents started to allow us to put our own touches on "our side" of the room. That one wall became our outlet for our room's creativity. It is known in our small circles as "the sticker wall." All of the stickers that my brother* *and I collected over the years have been placed on this wall. We were not allowed to change our room in any other way: no posters, no new paint color, no nail holes without the permission of our parents. However, this one wall was all ours to do with as we pleased. It was such a great way to express ourselves without drastically changing any other area of the room. My brother and I have grown up, moved out, and our old room has been repainted and remodeled to be a reading room, but that wall still stands just as it was years ago. To my mom, it is a reminder of the memories of us growing up—like a living scrapbook that never gets put away.*

5. To go along with the concept of doors never being locked, you have the right to walk into any room in your kingdom without permission. Your child's room is not, nor will it ever be, off limits to you. Just as the door on the frame is your possession, so is the room in which your child resides. "Get out of my room" is a phrase which should never be heard, and requires a consequence if uttered even once. When they ask for a reason why you are allowed to barge into their room but they aren't allowed in yours, your answer again is simple. "If you

would like to have 'some' privacy, and have me knock before I enter, some rent will be required." It will not take long for the child to understand that he doesn't need that much privacy; video games and movies are much more important to adolescents than a shut (and unlocked) bedroom door.

> **CHAD:** *When growing up, our bedroom door was NEVER locked. This was partly because my parents had installed doorknobs throughout the house that did not have locks on them, but also because we never shut any of the doors in our house except the bathroom. When I was very young and wanted a nightlight, my parents used the hallway light on a dimmer switch as my nightlight. The only way I could see that light was to leave my bedroom door open. I got so used to the concept that I felt almost claustrophobic when I got to college and started closing my door at night. The human brain has an amazing ability to become accustomed to almost anything; whatever you would like to see in your children can be achieved as long as you start early enough and follow through every time.*

6. If there is anything in your kingdom that must have

rules that are followed without question, it is technology. As we have said before, the computer is one of the most impressive and helpful creations we as a race have ever created and, unfortunately for parents and teachers, it is also one of the most dangerous. Technology in the right hands is a wonderful thing; however, in the hands of the inexperienced or naïve, it can prove to be serious and even life-threatening. Monitor your children's computer use often. If at all possible set up the computer, or have them use it, in a common room rather than in their bedroom. Ask them to help you understand whatever they are interested in: MySpace, Facebook, blogging, or video chatting. See how quickly they move from one site to another and get to know the workings of your home computer. When you see your children quickly hit a bunch of buttons as you enter the room, it's a good bet that they were closing something. Check the history after they finish using the computer, or look over their shoulder to see how many windows are open in the task bar at the bottom of the screen. It is extremely important that your children understand how vulnerable they are to predators when using the internet.

CHAD: *It's interesting to see how kids react in school* based on how I assume they would react at home to an "invasion of privacy." A few years ago, I had a student who was supposed to be researching for a project, and every time I walked around the computer lab and neared her area, she quickly grabbed for the mouse and clicked just before I got within view of her monitor. This went on for a couple of minutes. I did not tell her that I knew she was up to something, nor did I tell her to show me what was on the other screen that she had open in a different browser window. I simply played her game. I waited until she wasn't looking and turned off one of the computers behind her so that I could use that monitor as a mirror. Once I was on the other side of the room, I saw her change screens again and I could then see that she was playing a video game during research time. I waited a few minutes and made an announcement to the class reminding them that games were off limits. When I did this I looked directly at her and said her name. She said, "Me? I'm not playing games; I'm doing my research." I replied, "What are you researching? Hmm—Tetris, maybe?" She blushed and said, "How did you...?" I pointed to the monitor that I had *turned off and said "Reflections are amazing, aren't they?" and then I smiled. She knew she was busted but apologized and went back to actual research. I pulled her aside later and said, "You know I can't give you full credit for research today, right?" and she said, "Yup, I know...Sorry about the game!" and left with a smile on her face.*

7. The only rights that your children have in your house are the rights that you give to them. Use of TV, computer, video game system, phone, etc...are all subject to your approval, and all can be taken away at any time without a timeline of how long they will be unavailable. Even the type of language used in the house is a right that is earned. Foul language we have already covered, but sibling rivalry, bullying, name calling, or just saying words that you feel are unacceptable must not be tolerated even once. It is your house, and as such, you have a right to say what goes within its walls. Just because Timmy can say "that sucks" at his house doesn't mean that anyone will be able to in this house.

DIANE: *I don't know where the idea of sibling rivalry or bullying in your own family being normal came from, but most people seem to believe it. I'm* *sorry but it just makes my stomach hurt! Why in the world would you let your precious children be mean to each other, tease each other, or hit each other? I just don't get it! Your family members are the ones you should be able to count on for support and back-up, not be afraid of what they're going to do to you next. When Chad and Scott would start arguing over a toy, knowing that the situation could escalate, I would step in and say, "You can work this out together or the toy is gone...which do you want?" Well, they didn't want the toy to be gone, so usually they worked it out. Were they ecstatically happy? Of course not, but they did learn some reasoning power and control over their own emotions. If kids can learn to reconsider choices at home first, it becomes easier to deal with outsiders later. I'm not saying our boys never fought with each other, but since they did not have permission to, they spent much more of their time resolving their conflicts without violence.*

8. Okay...now here is one of those life-altering concepts that can make or break your child-rearing experience. Are you ready for it? "NOTHING YOU ARE DOING IN

THE MOMENT IS MORE IMPORTANT THAN YOUR CHILD'S FUTURE." Work is important in American culture; meetings are important; phone calls are important; deadlines are important; but are they as important to you as making sure that your children have the future you envision for them? Put down the cell phone, turn off the TV and spend time with your children. The more time you spend with your kids, getting to know them and what they like, the more time you have to impress upon them what you want for them, what you feel they are capable of, and what you expect of them. It will become internal over time…and here we are back to Pavlov again!

MYTH 6

THEY'LL FIX IT FOR ME

Think back to when you were a kid…if you forgot something at home that you needed for school, did you have the option of calling home? If so, would your parent actually bring up what you were missing? Even if all of this was true, did you receive full credit for whatever was missing? The average answer for all of the above is a resounding, "No!" If you got yourself into a jam when you were a kid, you were probably forced to find a solution to your problem and/or face the consequences. Too often in today's world parents want to shield their children so badly that it begins to hinder their growth and skew their perception of what life is really like. As a parent, you should want to help your child become the most responsible and well adjusted person he or she can be. But how can your children achieve this status without learning the lessons that life has to teach? How is your interference with the learning of these lessons going to impact their future?

1. Taking responsibility for your children's actions is a disservice to them and their future.

2. If you take the time to make everything an important learning lesson: it will be.

3. If parents ALWAYS fix their child's problems, it leads to a general lack of leaders for the future.

4. Forgetfulness is only corrected through negative consequences.

5. Work ethic is learned—teach it early.

6. Tough love is so-called for a reason—it's tough on the parents, not on the children.

7. Allow children to attempt to figure a way out of a problem before intervening.

8. Children must learn "when" to ask for help—NO crying wolf.

9. Choices will always have consequences—children must learn to take responsibility for their actions.

1. When it comes to kids taking responsibility for their actions, parents cannot start too soon. It may not seem like a big deal to bring your child's lunch to school when he forgets it at home; however, it just may be the worst thing that you can do as a parent. We know, being teachers ourselves, that you would do anything to help your child, but, "what am I helping them to become?" is the question that you should be asking yourself. Do you wish to help them become self-sufficient and responsible adults, or do you want to help enable them to become dependent upon others for even the simplest of life's tasks? Taking the responsibility out of your children's hands is a huge disservice; it forces them to believe that they are incapable of responsibility, which, as you can guess, is a very serious problem. So unless you are willing to bring your 40-year-old, live-at-home child his lunch at the workplace, let your children miss one or two lunches at school where their friends will provide for them and force them to believe that it is their responsibility to remember: lunches, homework, projects, permission slips, etc.

DIANE: *When I taught sixth grade, the teachers decided to be very strong about enforcing our responsibility requirements. At that time, we went on a field trip to a camp every year. We gave the kids their permission slips a week before the due date with reminders each day. We made sure they* *and their parents knew that if the slip was not turned in by the due date, the child would not go on the field trip. The first year, three kids were not allowed to go on the trip. The parents were not at all happy and tried to take all the blame. We reminded them that the kids would have had the slips signed if they had believed there were no rescues. The next year, all of the students did return their permission slips on time.*

2. Now that we are on the right track in fostering responsibility, it is important to note that you must continue to teach that lesson in any and all situations. It only takes one time of "bailing your child out" to undo all that they have learned about responsibility. Consistency is the glue that will bind your child to the lessons that will teach him or her to succeed in life, and you, as the parent, must take responsibility to teach this lesson.

CHAD: *I had a pair of twins in class recently who could not be any more different. One was always on time; the other was always late. One was always talking; the other quiet as a mouse. One always turning in her assignments on time; the other...a little less often. On one particular occasion a project was due. I was making my rounds to check the work in and make sure that they had something to show* *for the due date. When I got to the first of these twins, she showed me a project that looked nice and was completed according to the rubric. When I got to the other twin and asked to see what she had, she said, "My mom is bringing it up now." I started to move on and then stopped and looked back at the first twin. "Didn't you ride to school today with your sister and her giant poster?" "Yes." "How did you 'forget' your project then?" "I don't know, my mom forgot to remind me." "So whose responsibility is this project, you or your mom?" I asked and then I smiled at her to let her know I was not mad at her; I just needed to make a point.*

3. Not to beat a dead horse, but whose job is it to teach children the lessons that allow them to succeed? Imagine what the world would be like if Einstein's parents fought his teachers to get his grades up so that he could graduate. (Einstein never graduated from high school, but because he followed his passion, he became one of the world's greatest physicists). What if Thomas Edison's family and friends let him give up after failing the first time when trying to invent the light bulb? (It took him over one thousand attempts.) It is only through adversity that we are able to conquer the human condition. The obstacles that we face along our journey shape and mold us into the people that we become, and without these

obstacles we remain the same people we were in grade school—dependent to a fault. The world needs leaders-strong individuals who work through problems and can reason through adversity. These kinds of leaders are more common that you might think; however, their numbers are dwindling as our youth find ways to manipulate the role of parents.

DIANE: *I learned a life lesson in taking responsibility for my actions when I was about eight. I lived only a few blocks from my elementary school, and everyone walked to and from school and walked home every day for lunch. Naturally, we often walked with the same kids. One sloppy, fall day we had all worn our boots to school, but many of us were carrying them home at lunchtime with plans to leave them there. Teasing, fooling around, pushing, shoving, giggling and then...I did it! I grabbed Terry's boots out of his hand and threw them in the swamp we were passing. I ran home and ate my lunch, with my heart in my throat. We lived a block apart and our parents were good friends. Would Terry tell his mom; what about the other kids who saw?*

Sure enough, my mom received a phone call and after hanging up asked, "So, how was your walk home today?"

I gulped and stuttered, "Umm...fine."

My mom said, "That was your teacher. She said Terry's mom called her about an incident on the way home...anything you want to tell me now?"

I moaned, "Oh, no...I'm sorry. I don't know why I didn't tell you. I threw Terry's boots in the pond! I'm sorry!"

My stomach was a mess! I had done something really stupid and then lied to my mom. What would happen now? My mother guided me through the process of choosing my own punishment. I was made to go get Terry's boots, apologize to him, apologize to my teacher, and tell my dad the truth. That was all very hard for an eight-year-old. I don't remember if or what the further punishment may have been, but the memories and the guilt from that long ago event have been long-lasting.

4. You would be amazed at how often the word "forgot" is used in today's classrooms. There must be a nationwide epidemic of forgetfulness! What's interesting to note is that no matter how many times you say, "This will be the last time I...," it's not until you actually follow through with that threat that your child will learn the lesson. Forgetfulness is a misnomer. In fact, it is not being

forgetful that leaves your children with no homework to turn in; it is laziness. And the way to curb laziness is through the use of negative consequences. If something bad happens to you, naturally you will do what you can to keep it from happening again…unless someone else is willing to do it for you. Humans are designed to take the path of least resistance; in other words, we do whatever is easiest. And believe us…kids will always try to get away with doing what is easier. Unfortunately, to learn the lesson of forgetfulness, you have to fail a few times. And parents, you must let them fail now in order for them to succeed in life.

CHAD: *One afternoon my dad took us to a family friend's house and told us to bring along a few toys to play with while we were there. I thought that this would be the perfect time to have all of my favorites to play with, so I loaded all of my best toys into the back of a Keebler Elf semi truck that was just big enough to ride. When it was almost time to go, my dad told my brother and me to get all of our stuff and get ready to go, but we were having too much fun in the pool to pay attention to his directions. A few minutes later, I had totally forgotten what he had told me to do. Then, we heard the infamous whistle. We jumped out of the pool and ran to the car, waving goodbye over our shoulders on the way.*

Just before we got home, I remembered that I had left my toys at the house. I knew that it was my fault for not listening to my dad, and so I didn't say anything. I remember being so mad, but surprisingly I was mad at myself for not listening. I lost all of my best toys because I forgot to grab what I thought was most important. I found out later that the kids at the house thought I had left them as a present and were so excited that they later wrote me a thank-you letter. That letter helped me to see that those toys were much more important to them than they were to me anymore.

5. Teaching work ethic to children when they are older is infinitely harder than teaching it to them when they are young. Children in today's school systems simply do not try as hard as in generations past. This is partly because they know that their parents will bail them out when their grade is not an A; however, it's not just the bail-out, it's a general lack of expectations on the part of older generations. We expect less of our children today, which leads to that sense of entitlement that we talked about earlier. You should never expect anything less than the absolute best from your kids; you should demand it. It's not to say that they have to be the absolute best in any given task, but they MUST do THEIR absolute best. Whether it's a project for school or a play on the field, the

amount of effort that your child puts into anything that he or she does will speak volumes about not only the kind of person he is, but also the kind of parents who raised him.

CHAD: *I hated Saturdays when I was a kid. Seems like a strange thing for a kid to dislike, right? Here's why: Saturday was my dad's work day; - the time he had to get everything around the house done. Being a kid, all I wanted to do on Saturday morning was eat cereal and watch morning cartoons, but that was not the household that I grew up in.*

Saturday mornings I would wake up and before I could get my first bowl of cereal down, my dad would call in from the garage, "Hey Diane, send the boys out when they get up."

There could be any number of things that needed to get done: cutting the grass, raking the leaves, home improvement projects, working on cars, changing oil, etc. There was ALWAYS something to get done on Saturday. At the time I hated it, but looking back on it now, I couldn't be happier about those Saturdays. It instilled within me a work ethic that I carry with me to this day. It also gave me a lot of time with my parents- time to get to know them and what they believe...time that you can't get back later!

6. If this all seems a little heartless…well, that's okay. It should seem a little heartless to a parent. Parental instincts are genetically hardwired into our genes, and to go against what you "want" to do in order to help your child in the moment is difficult, but it is very necessary in order to instill in them what will help them in the future. It's called tough love not because it's tough on the children (remember, children are VERY resilient), but because it's tough on the parents. Discipline is not just a term to describe what happens to your child…it must also describe what you will have to possess in order to raise your children to become the responsible, productive members of society that you know they can be. Be tough as a parent and in time your children will thank you for it.

CHAD: *It wasn't until we started writing this book that I ever knew my mom had a hard time disciplining my brother and me when we were kids. Once we got talking, she told me how hard it was to punish us and how much it hurt her, but that she knew it was what was best for us. I also found out that she did not know that I appreciated the way I was raised. I thanked her for everything she did when I was younger, and it was the first time she knew for sure that she did it right…it only took 31 years!! Sometimes the gratification takes longer than we would like, but it makes it that much more special* *when it does finally happen.*

7. Growing up is hard…it always has been and it always will be. It's supposed to be hard. If everything in life were easy, no one would try to better themselves or better the world around them. When children have problems, their first instinct is to go to someone who may be able to fix that problem for them…that would be you! If you are able to step back from the situation and see that it could be used as a learning experience before automatically fixing the problem in order to make your child happy, it will pay off in the end. Learning how to solve your problems as a child is an invaluable lesson. It prepares the child not only for his school years, but also for the challenges he will face throughout life. When very young children are fighting over a toy, most parents take the toy away or tell one of them to stop and give the toy to the other child. Why not hold the toy as collateral until the two children figure out a solution? (i.e. - I will share it with him/ I will play with it now and he will get it later). It's the ability to solve problems on your own that will determine how far you can go in society, because there will come a day when you are on your own and no one will be able to help you. Don't you want your child to be prepared for that day?

CHAD: *When I was in seventh grade, I accidentally offended a really big girl in my band class. I was*

4'11" and she was easily 5'10"! She got up in my face and told me she was going to beat me up, and I told her she was full of it (probably not my best move). Over the course of the next couple weeks, she kept harassing me and pushing me in the back in the hallways. I was beginning to get scared that she wasn't going to let it go. I went to my mom for help and she told me to try to work it out on my own. She also said that if it got any worse I should go talk to the principal or one of my teachers and let her know each day how it was going. Unbeknownst to me, this was extremely difficult for her not to be able to help me when I desperately needed it. After a couple of weeks of being pushed in the back, I snapped, swung around and yelled at this girl, "I'm tired of getting hit in the back. If you want to hit me, man up and hit me in the face instead of these stupid cheap shots!" She balled her fist and got ready to hit while I went into panic mode knowing I was about to get punched in the face. Before she could throw her punch, her older brother, who had seen the altercation, came up and stopped her. The brother told her that it was impressive for someone so small to stand up for himself and told her to leave me alone from then on. He nodded at me and that was the end of it. I never heard from her again. I learned a very valuable lesson about standing up for myself and facing fears—a lesson I would not have learned had my mom taken action before I truly needed it.

8. Knowing when to help your children and when to allow them to create a solution on their own will be one of the hardest lines to decipher. Sometimes children may be in over their heads and not know it. Sometimes they are fully capable of handling the situation themselves but will ask for help because it makes their life or their decision easier. When your child asks you to "help them" on a school project, make sure that you are doing just that... helping. As teachers, we see projects all year long that were "helped" to make them look more professional or more sophisticated. It is not in your child's best interest to teach them that the work that they can do by themselves is not acceptable. Whatever the project looks like when your child is finished with it, as long as it's his personal best, it is perfect. But when your child truly does not know how to work through a problem or a scenario, it is up to you to help guide him through it. Most of the problems that your child will encounter that will require help from you will have to do with emotional pain or change. All kids can figure out how to make a project better if you just give them enough time and coaxing, but not all kids can figure out what to do after their first boyfriend or girlfriend breaks their heart.

DIANE: *When Chad was in fifth grade, he was given an assignment for his social studies class. He had to make an "America the Beautiful" book using stanzas of the song in his own handwriting and cut-out pictures to illustrate each one. The presentation was also very important. Chad started looking at the song and writing the stanzas and looking through books for pictures. When it came time to organize the book, he asked for ideas. I was happy to give him suggestions on different ways to lay things out or which photos I liked best for certain stanzas, but Chad did all the actual work himself. I sat with him a lot while he was putting the whole thing together, talking about both the project and other things. He asked, when he was done, if I would help him get the cover laminated so it would look better. I took him with me to school and showed him how the laminator worked. He was very proud of the work he did because it truly was his work. Try not to give your kids so much help that they begin to believe they are incapable of doing any work on their own.*

9. Once your children are on the right path, making the right decisions, working to the best of their abilities, and asking for help only when they truly need it, your job as a parent becomes easier but is by no means finished. All choices come with consequences; usually good decisions

come with positive consequences and vice versa. However, every once in a while there is a choice that needs to be made that will not have favorable consequences no matter how delicately the decision is executed. This is when your child will need your guidance and wisdom the most. It's not about always making the "right choice;" it's about making the "best choice" under the given circumstances. That is the choice that your children need to know you expect them to make every time.

MYTH 7

IT'S NEVER MY FAULT

One of the most commonly used phrases uttered by children is the infamous, "But it's not my fault…" Unfortunately, it is also one of the most dangerous to let slide. Children who truly believe that it's never their fault tend to get into trouble more often because in their minds it does not reflect on them personally. As a parent or teacher, you must look at what they are doing and make sure that they always take responsibility for their own actions when they are young. This allows for them to internalize that lesson and begin to make it part of their personality. When you look back on your childhood, it's interesting to think about what you tried to get away with while pinning the blame on someone or something else. Fortunately for us, the parents of the past liked to force us to learn our lessons the hard way…it was called "taking your lumps." Every now and then we get the opportunity to realize that our parents might actually have known what they were doing!

1. "I didn't do it" is a lie...it was a choice.

2. Consequences MUST be experienced in order to have an impact.

3. The difference between supporting your child and backing your child.

4. Excuses are disguises for poor work ethic.

5. Questioning, instead of yelling, will lead to independence.

6. ALWAYS side with authority figures on trivial issues.

7. Irresponsibility can become a lifelong disability.

8. Fault is no longer part of our vocabulary... replaced by "choice."

9. ALL people can learn from consistent expectations regardless of age, intelligence, or personal history.

10. "Learning disabilities" are not to be used as excuses but as opportunities to strive for more.

1. Children, like most people, will do nearly anything they can to keep from getting into trouble. We are programmed to avoid punishment at all cost; however, those punishments also serve a purpose. They help us to learn and grow as individuals. When children learn that "I didn't do it" is a phrase that works, they also learn to repeat it over and over again. The problem with that phrase is that they learn to use it when it's not true—this is called a lie. Everything that we do as individuals is a choice and we need to teach our children that honesty is always the best policy. Teaching children not to lie is definitely an art form, considering we've already told you to allow your kids to use you as an excuse if they want to get out of something that they feel is unsafe or wrong. However, this does not include lying to your family—there must remain a boundary that absolutely cannot be crossed. Family is the one thing that your children must not ever take for granted; the one group in which your child must have one hundred percent faith.

CHAD: *When I was a very small boy (still carrying around a tooth fairy pillow with a built-in pocket), I remember very clearly an incident I had that involved lying and not listening to my parents'* *directions. My brother and I shared a room growing up and one night my dad got home late and brought us a surprise for the morning. We were still awake so he gave us the present that night; it was a little thing of tic tacs. He told us VERY clearly not to eat them until the following day and to go to sleep. As soon as he left the room, Scott and I starting eating the tic tacs until they were all gone! When my dad came back up the stairs he could hear the tic tacs rattling in their container. He came back into our room and asked us if we had been eating any of them, and of course not wanting to get into trouble, we said no (even though the whole room smelled like spearmint). He pulled the tic tacs out of the pillow pocket and saw that they were all gone and was furious! Were we punished? Absolutely! Was it worth getting that angry over missing tic tacs? I believe it was because I did learn a valuable lesson about telling the truth that night.*

2. How many times were you told as a child not to do something and then went ahead and did it anyway? The answer for most people is quite a few times! Why is it that even though we were warned, even though we knew

it would turn out badly, we did it anyway? The answer is,because that's the only way we truly learn. People learn through experience and a lesson is not fully learned until the experience is undergone first hand. So although we, as parents or teachers, want to shield our children from the hurt and pain that we know the world has in store for them, we must remember to allow them to experience some of the minor pain and heartache for themselves so that they can learn from the experience and grow as people.

CHAD: *My brother and I were always looking for a new adventure, and we were always trying to build something new growing up. One of the endeavors that we undertook was the creation of a rope swing from our backyard tree. We asked our parents— okay, we begged our parents—to let us make a rope swing. They told us that it probably wasn't our best idea and that someone could get hurt, but said if we promised to wear our hockey helmets while swinging we could give it a try. We used small mooring rope for docking row boats, tied a slip knot and climbed to the top of an overhanging branch. We used a sturdy stick as a hand hold and after many "tests"* *began swinging!! It was GREAT! We had SO much fun; right up until its disastrous failure. I was at the highest point in the pendulum swing motion when the rope we used frayed and snapped. I went flying backward and landed on the edge of the lake we grew up on. Was I okay? Yes, except for one broken finger, I was fine. Was it the best idea we ever had? No, but it was a great learning experience and I wouldn't trade it for the world now. My brother and I learned so much from our mistakes growing up, and we are better "handymen" and "weekend warriors" because we were allowed to learn for ourselves how things worked.*

3. As we have discussed, what you should want more than anything in the entire world is to support your children in their quests to become fulfilled and productive members of society. The key word in that phrase though is "support." There is a difference between supporting your children and backing them. To support your children, you give them the tools necessary to achieve in life, which sometimes means that they must take responsibility for their actions when the consequences are less than optimal. What we as teachers see more often in today's

world though is a "backing" of children that strips them of the sense of responsibility that they MUST possess to become productive in today's world. Backing children can most often be seen in small issues such as leaving homework at home on a due date. In years past, parents would have let the child suffer the consequences of taking an "E" on a simple homework assignment in hopes that the lesson learned would be that they would be much more responsible next time. Now, however, on a daily basis we see children who ask to call their parents to bring them a forgotten lunch, homework, project, etc. These children usually follow up the question as to whether or not they can call home with, "It's okay. My mom doesn't mind." As parents and teachers, we need to make sure that our children experience some negative consequences in order to learn. To support our children, we may come up with a system that helps them to remember or a routine that keeps them from being forgetful.

> **DIANE:** *A plan that seemed to work for us involved getting organized the night before. All homework, notes, instruments, etc., are put in or next to backpacks which are placed near the back door and ready to go. Lunches are put in the backpack*

in the morning after being made (sorry, but I never gave up that chore), but all other stress-inducing activities are handled before bed. Clothes choices are set and ready to go. Jackets, hats, mittens, boots, and whatever else are put in place by the back door. This plan definitely reduces morning stress, but you must start the evening "rigamarole" sooner so that there is still calming down time before bed.

4. Work ethic is not a term that holds much credence in today's society. There was a time not too long ago when the work ethic that you put into your job, homework, or family was the most important judge of your character. We feel that this concept has been lost over time. In today's world of cell phones, internet, and online trading, people have become so used to instant gratification that the sense of accomplishment from a job well done has been replaced by the ease of "phoning a friend," consulting with the web, or ordering online. When it comes to kids, this trend is even more magnified. Today's children grew up in a globalized world of group sharing, and the internet has, in a sense, established a group mindset that proclaims that since the group is better or smarter than the individual, the individual effort is secondary to the overall result. In

schools, there have always been excuses for lack of work, but it has escalated to a point where students today will turn in projects that should have taken a week to finish with no more than one night's worth of work (the night before it's due, of course).

> **DIANE:** *Most teachers hand out "rubrics" or listed requirements for students to use on their own projects. Many students lose the rubric, make up their own requirements (often doing a beautiful job, by the way) and can't understand how they get a low grade.*
>
> *Teachers should be concerned with students doing their very best on everything. Unfortunately the educational system has been overpowered by data-driven accountability, forcing teachers to use tools like rubrics, which can be and often are the root of poor work ethic. We need to teach our children that doing their best is much more important than completing the minimum requirements expected. Even in today's strange work environment, doing a great job on the wrong project does not make up for doing an incomplete job on the assigned project.*

5. Children, much like adults, respond to positive reinforcements much more readily than to negative consequences. Think about your job--how do you feel if your boss shows up to your office or desk yelling and pointing fingers while blaming you for whatever went wrong? After your boss is finished with his or her tirade, do you feel like working harder or better? Probably not! Neither do your kids after being berated. In order to reach your children on an emotional level, you must give to them what you would expect from an employer. In that same work scenario, what if your boss had come to you and asked to sit down, showed you the numbers that were presented to him or her and asked you to explain what was going on? Would you be more willing to reason with your boss and find a solution that would be mutually beneficial? The answer is probably yes. If you want your children's behavior to change, you need to let them know why you want it to change. There are, of course, exceptions, like running toward the road, in which case an explanation is not prescribed since there is not time, but even then it would benefit the child and your relationship to explain that the reason you "flipped out" was because you were scared for their safety. The explanation is what allows the child to understand that it is not a personal attack, but instead the reaction of a parent who truly cares about making the child's life a better one. One of the ways in which parents and teachers can utilize this emotional connection is to ask their children what they did wrong. Making children vocalize what they did forces them to think about not only what they did but why they did it. Again, it's about being down on their level and controlling the conversation by not losing your cool.

> **DIANE:** *Often as a teacher on the playground, I'd have two or three students come running up tattling on each other about something. In these cases, it was extremely important for me to have each child individually tell me what "he" did—no interrupting and no telling what the other kids did. It's amazing the truth that comes out that way. It starts with "Johnny was hitting me." And ends with "I was pushing Johnny." Make each child accountable for his own actions.*

6. In life, people are forced to wear many different hats. We conduct ourselves differently based on who we are surrounded by as well as where we find ourselves. Most of us act completely differently around our friends than we do around our bosses or colleagues. What may be okay for

your family to do in the privacy of your own home may not be something you choose to let the rest of the world see. School is much like the different facets of your life. What may be okay for the students to do in one classroom may not be acceptable in another - let alone what students are able to do at home versus at school. This is a very tough lesson to learn and it is becoming even more difficult in the society in which we find ourselves. It is vitally important for parents to side with authority figures on any and all trivial issues. What is a trivial issue? Anything that isn't going to drastically influence the outcome of the child's life. Children MUST learn that authority figures are truly the ones in control, and that Mommy and Daddy aren't ALWAYS going to be able to fix everything. Without this lesson, children learn that there are no consequences for any actions, which can become a very dangerous concept when they reach maturity.

DIANE: *A friend had been to a parenting class and was feeling much stronger about her abilities in that area. She proudly told me about an incident with her daughter in the middle school. The school had a policy of no gum chewing, and her daughter was caught chewing gum. After being warned* *three separate times, she was given an after-school detention. My friend was appalled because "That is a stupid rule!" She complained to the school and was told that all children must adhere to school rules. So...deciding to back her daughter, she went to a doctor and got a medical release so her daughter could chew gum in school! Arghhh! What did she teach her daughter as a life skill? Do whatever you want, and Mom will get you out of it. Rules don't apply.*

7. Responsibility is such a key issue facing the world today. The idea that people must be responsible for their actions is one that can change the course of human history for the positive or for the negative. Children who do not believe that they are responsible for their own actions are children who will grow up believing that the rules of society do not apply to them. It's hard as a parent or teacher to think about the time when your children will "leave the nest" and set out into the world all on their own, but that is the picture that you must keep in your head. What kind of person do you want to see your child become? Irresponsibility at a young age can actually become a debilitating disability. As teachers we are able

to see the result of this type of mentality. Unfortunately, this responsibility is not something that can be fixed easily later in life, so it is crucial that you instill this quality in your children while they are still young.

CHAD: *A few years ago, I had a student in class who was just a ray of sunshine. Great personality, always smiling, always saying please and thank you. In fact, the only downfall for this particular student was her immense lack of responsibility. She came to show me her new phone one afternoon; she was sooo excited. The very next day she came up to me laughing and showed me this hunk of plastic that used to be a phone…she had dropped it and then kicked it into traffic walking home. She laughed at herself and told me it was okay because her mom was going out that day to buy her a new one. Less than a week later she showed me a cracked screen on her new, new phone! She had sat on it at the movies and didn't notice that her keys were in the same pocket. She laughed again and told me that her mom was going to get a new one for her over the weekend. This student showed me five new phones in the course of one school year! Five free phones!! She took no pride in* *her possessions because everything she had would be replaced if need be. She never had to pay a cent for her new phones despite being given an allowance weekly. Her parents had inadvertently instilled a disability within her: a total lack of responsibility.*

8. How many times have you heard from your children, "It's not my fault"? This is one of those phrases that we feel is unacceptable. Claiming that something is not your fault is just another way of saying that I refuse to accept responsibility for what I have done. We have chosen to replace "fault" with "choice" in our classrooms. Everything we do is a choice; whether it's what we wear to school in the morning or what friends we keep, every single thing we do is a choice. If your children have a hard time taking responsibility, make them use the word "choice" instead of "fault" and they will begin to see that it doesn't even make sense to claim that it wasn't his or her choice (because almost 100 percent of the time it is). This takes perseverance on your part as the parent or teacher, but if you can get children to believe that everything they do is a choice, their behavior will change naturally over time.

CHAD: *One of the most readily used excuses in my district is that of the athlete. In the small community* *in which I teach, the majority of students are active in sports. Too often though, they try to use that as an excuse. There are countless times each year that I hear from a student, "I couldn't finish my homework because I was at soccer practice and by the time I got home my mom made me go to bed." I don't know about you, but I played soccer and I can guarantee that soccer practice does not go until 10 o'clock at night (which is when many of them have said that they get off the internet or off the phone with friends). This is an excuse and nothing more; therefore, it must be treated in the same manner as someone who came in and said, "I forgot to do my homework." Sports should never be used as an excuse not to do school work. School is their primary job, and sports need to be kept secondary. If students don't have enough time to finish their homework, then maybe they're too busy to be participating in sports.*

9. Probably the most important part of our whole teaching and parenting style is consistency. Once you can remain consistent, your children can and will learn. Scientists have been able to teach a mouse to finish a maze,

a chimp to pilot a spacecraft, and a gorilla to spell using sign language all through the effective use of consistent behavior modification. Your children are no different; in fact, they are smarter. All people can learn at high levels as long as those responsible for teaching have the patience and perseverance to see it through. Do not do your children the disservice of taking their ability to learn away from them by fixing everything for them.

DIANE: *I had a fifth grade student who "knew" he was a poor student. Paul didn't like school, but was a very nice kid. He thought he was awful at math even though he came from a family with a business everyone helped with. He used money all the time but hadn't connected school math with home math. As soon as I told him how good he was, he began to shine. He started to smile more and find confidence in himself. Encouraging people to be their best is not the same as saying "good job" to someone who has not done a good job. Self-esteem comes from inside, not from outside.*

10. Learning disabilities is one of those topics that is very touchy to talk about in our modern society of political correctness and instant gratification. Are there

students who are truly learning disabled and need extra help? Absolutely, and we do not want to do anything to take away from the programs that strive to help these students. However, is there a separate group of students who manipulate the system in order to make "learning" easier on them? Yes. Special education is a very intricate piece in the education system and our students could not be as successful without it. A caution should accompany special education, though. Sometimes it may be more beneficial for students to be forced to "push through" their limitations and fears to discover that they can actually do it on their own. This discovery has the ability to be much more effective than any amount of time spent with a special education specialist. Having a disability should never be an excuse to quit.

MYTH 8
EVERYBODY DOES IT

For generations, a single phrase could be heard coming from the mouths of parents when trying to make their children understand why doing some particular action was stupid or dangerous. That phrase was, "If all your friends jumped off a bridge, would you?" The only problem with this phrase is that in our world of X-games, extreme sports, and instant gratification, the answer would most likely be, "Yes!" Children today do not equate jumping off a bridge with any kind of danger…in fact, if they were given the choice to watch their friend bungee jumping from that bridge or actually take the plunge themselves, the majority of them would try it. Children today have a group mindset; from the time that they were very young they have been taught to work together, having grown up with the internet, which makes the concept of hoarding information obsolete. Information sharing is the way of the future and because of this the mentality to do what "everybody else" is doing is very dangerous and a real possibility. In order to ensure that your children can make decisions for themselves, as well as become the responsible and productive adults that we want them to be, it is critical for them to believe that just because everybody does it does not mean that it's right.

1. Update the bridge that "everybody" is jumping off.

2. Friends vs. cliques

3. Children learn at a VERY young age that it's easier to follow the herd.

4. Self- thinking problems vs. herd mentality problems

5. Only have one chance in life to make the right choices the first time

6. "I don't know why I did that" can be an honest answer from children.

7. Definition of Respect, Integrity, and Honor

8. "Everybody does it" goes for parents too.

9. Children are malleable—shape them into the people you want them to be.

10. Trust in people is a rare commodity in today's society.

1. For years, parents and teachers have used the scenario of a friend jumping off a bridge to symbolize something dangerous and stupid. Unfortunately for this little gem, times have changed. In today's world of action sports, jumping off a bridge not only seems like a decent idea but it may seem like the adventure of a lifetime. Parents in today's world not only need to know what they want their children to become but how to get them there. Parents and teachers must understand the psyche of their child. The bridge that our children are to be jumping from needs to be updated to reflect something that they still consider to be dangerous or stupid. "If all your friends stole a car, would you?" "If all your friends shot someone, would you?" This technique is twofold. First, parents and teachers must really know their children in order to give them scenarios that make sense to them. Just because it was done a certain way in the past doesn't necessarily mean that it will work today. Second, parents and teachers must know what they do and do not want their children to participate in. The bottom line is that parents and teachers need to truly know their children, so spend time getting to know them.

DIANE: *I must admit, as a parent, I was often tempted*

to go with the, "Because I told you!" option. I tried not to use it, but it takes more thinking to come up with an alternate plan. You need to come up with some ideas to use before you need them. I'm sure if the boys had tried to use an, "Everybody's doing it" routine on me, I probably would have put on my game face, raised my eyebrows, and said something like, "But I only care about you!" A discussion could then ensue, but they would know that the bottom line was just me, caring about them.

2. For as long as there has been school there have been cliques. You remember those groups from high school, don't you? There were the cool kids, the jocks, the nerds, etc. These groups are called cliques because it is superficiality that defines them and not their loyalty to one another. Friends, on the other hand, are defined as such because they are there for you no matter what group you are a part of or why. "Everybody does it" is a phrase that leads children toward cliques and away from true friendship. The danger in this is the ability for cliques to lead children to do things that the cliques will approve of only because it is someone else doing the action. Kids have an astounding ability to be cruel to one another, and this kind of bullying

can be seen every day from elementary playgrounds to the locker room in high school. However, once in a blue moon, we get the opportunity to see someone standing up for that person who is being bullied despite what the group will think of them. This is the child that we want to commend. This is the child who will grow up to make positive decisions and become a productive member of society. This is what you should want from your child.

CHAD: *I had a student during my first year of teaching who really reached out to me. This student was exceptionally bright and good-hearted. She went so far as to invite me to her karate banquet despite being part of a class that I was constantly yelling at (remember, it was my first year teaching). Years later, I was walking through the halls at the high school and saw this young lady talking with friends and she seemed upset. When I went to say hello, I found out that during the school day there was a group of guys bullying a smaller freshman student who was unable to stand up for himself. This good-hearted former student of mine stepped in and yelled at the group of guys (even threatening them), and even though many of her close friends were part of the* *same clique as those guys, she disregarded what her friends "might" think of her and did what she felt in her heart was right. I found out later that many of her friends who refused to stand up for the bullied boy earlier went on to tell the guys in the group to quit being so immature. You never know what effect you will have on a clique when you stand up for what is truly right.*

3. Our society reveres its heroes for their ability to lead and for their ability to get others to trust in them enough to give up control. The dilemma we face with this is that our leaders are not born to lead; instead they learn how to lead over time through a series of positive and negative reinforcements. What we see with children is the beginning signs of this hierarchy of leader versus follower. If given the choice, nearly all parents and teachers would choose to have their children become leaders instead of followers, and the reason behind this is that the leader is true to his or herself and cannot be swayed from that path, while the follower can be manipulated. In childhood, the fear of ridicule or abandonment from "friends" is a very powerful motivator to become just one in the herd instead of being the lone shepherd. To get your children

to become leaders, they must have a VERY strong sense of who they are and what is right.

CHAD: *Children have an amazing ability to force status quo upon their peers. In one of the districts in which I worked, I noticed this trend was not only prevalent but was running rampant with no sign of stopping. There have been a handful of students that I have taught who have wanted to make a drastic change in their lives and in their schooling. These students were labeled the class clowns, but after a semester of instruction from new teachers who placed a significant importance on being the real you, these students began to want to make a change. They started answering questions in class, turning in homework, and studying for tests. Unfortunately, their classmates knew them only as the class clowns, so as they tried to make the switch from class clown to academic student they met with a great deal of resistance from their friends. Even when teachers were able to get through to these students for a short time, I found out later that the majority of them resumed their class clown personas once high school began. To be able to instill the idea of true self in our* *children is a goal which we all, teachers and parents together, should strive for.*

4. After reading the last section, you may be asking yourself how to combat the ridicule that leaders face early on. The short answer is that there is no way to combat the ridicule, but there is a way to combat its effect on your child. It is true that if you teach your child to become a leader he or she will deal with a certain degree of bullying or name calling. What you have to ask yourself though is whether or not it's worth a little ridicule in order to prepare them to reach their full potential later in life. Remember, it is your job to give them everything you can to make their lives easier and more fulfilling…a little name calling in childhood is nothing when compared to the satisfaction that comes from a lifetime of leadership and decency. No matter what direction your child chooses, there will always be some kind of obstacle to overcome. The real question is do you want the instant gratification that being part of the herd provides, or do you want the long-lasting satisfaction that leadership qualities provide?

DIANE: *I grew up with the last name of Horn…think I had some teasing?? Oh, yes! "Horny" and "Toot-toot" often. When I got married, I gained the name*

Finkbeiner—Whoa—besides silly name-calling by friends, other people, including children in classes at school, couldn't say the name correctly. So, as Chad and Scott were growing up, we teased them constantly on purpose for fun so that name-calling would mean nothing to them. When your parents say Punkinhead, Turkeybutt, Shrinkbutter, and Knucklenose all day long in an endearing manner, it's much harder to be upset when your friends or classmates try to tease you with weird names.

5. "You never get a second chance to make a first impression" is as true today as it was when it was first uttered centuries ago. When we teach our kids that first impressions are important, and that no matter what we would like to believe, those impressions determine who you are in others' eyes. As a society, we like to tell ourselves that initial impressions should be repressed until we get to know the people we are judging better; however, this ideal situation just plain goes against our natural animal instincts. Humans have relied on their instincts for preservation and evolution for eons. Children need to know that following everyone else and their ideas may allow them to be categorized before they have even had

a chance to prove themselves or their worth in another's eyes. Because once that trust is gone, it takes ten times longer to win it back. In school, this may not be all that important, but when that first impression is for a college recruiter or an interviewer for a new job, it is essential.

DIANE: *Remember that making first impressions goes both ways. As well as making good first impressions themselves, children need to be aware of the impressions others make on them. Children who have clear thoughts of who they are need to be aware of who other people are before giving complete trust. Stacy, a strong leader-type, forgot all her strengths when Brandon caught her eye. She became a follower of only Brandon without waiting to see his true value. Children need to be taught when very young to trust slowly. Once you think they have learned the lessons you want them to have, don't give up on the reminders.*

6. It is amazing how much science is able to teach us about our behavior, but at the same time it is amazing to see that with all of our scientific advancements we still don't know why kids act the way they do. There is a time in a child's life when his hormones and intellect are

in such disproportion that he truly does things without thinking. We have all witnessed children doing something that they absolutely know is wrong and when we ask them why they did it, their answer is a simple and humble "I don't know." Under most circumstances this infuriates the rational mind of parents and teachers; however, we must understand that there are some very rare cases when this is an honest answer. This is when explanation works much more effectively than yelling. In the child's mind, he truly doesn't even know why he performed that action: knowing that his actions disappointed you or scared you is much more powerful than knowing that it made you mad enough to yell at him. Remember to reinforce what it is you want from your children, without losing your temper, to maximize your effectiveness.

CHAD: *I had a student not too long ago who turned in a project that I later found had parts of it that were plagiarized. This was after I had given him an extension due to a sports injury he had sustained. He asked if he could have one more day to finish just the typing of the project because it was already done, but with his broken bone he was unable to type fast enough to finish the project on time. I gave* *him the extra day he had asked for, but I made him promise me that the work was done already. To make sure that this was the case, I also told him that he had to bring a letter from home stating that he did not do any more work on the project except typing from his draft. It turns out the project was not done at all, and he finished it in one night (by copying and pasting from internet sites). The letter that came in from his parent was my first red flag as it said nothing about being done already, and when I confronted him about the plagiarism I found, I asked if he had copied anything and he said no. I showed him his project with the internet sites stapled to it and the passages highlighted, and I told him again that I was going to give him one more chance to tell the truth and again he stuck with his story. It wasn't until I got him one-on-one out in the hallway that he was able to come clean. I asked him why he had lied; why he didn't just tell me the truth off the bat and he said……that's right, the famous "I don't know." He didn't want to lie to me, but he was already too deep in the lie to come clean and save face. A punishment was given, but it was not as harsh as it could have been because we struck a bargain that day. He looked me in the eyes and swore never to lie to me again. That respect helped forge a bond that still lasts to this day.*

7. Your children knowing what you expect of them and what you expect for them is very effective in guiding their behavior. What we really want for our kids is the best life possible. To gain that life, they must learn not to follow the crowd when that crowd is headed in a direction that is in direct opposition to their own moral compass that has been provided by parents and teachers. Children must understand the words that parents and teachers use. If a parent says to their young child that he or she is expected to be respectful, it means nothing if the child does not know what the word means. As a parent or teacher, you need to be able to explain your expectations to your children in words that they understand for it to be useful in their upbringing.

> **CHAD:** *On the first day of school every year I tell my students what it is that will be expected of them in my classroom. There are four words on my board all year long; those words are my pillars of character that my students are expected to follow. The words I choose to put my faith in are, "Respect, Integrity,*

Work Ethic, and Honor." I tell the students that this is the only thing I expect from them during the entire year, but I know that many of my students do not know what these words mean. I give them a chance to look over the words for a while and think about what they might mean, and then I go through a discussion with the classes about what they think each word might mean. Once I have all of their ideas, I tell them what they mean to me and how I expect that they will be used in class. This detail is key because I point to those words during class when someone is being disrespectful as a warning before I discipline anyone.

8. "Everybody does it" is a double-edged sword. There are so many parents in today's world that are guilty of falling for this same logic. More parents today than ever before are concerned with their appearance. Wanting to be the "cool mom" or the "fun dad" has led to an increase in herd mentality for parents as well as children. There are times when, as a parent, you would like to make a good impression for your children, but this is a very counterproductive mentality. The first impression is only important when it aligns with your moral compass

or your overall ethics. Having your child's friends think of you as the cool parent is usually your first clue that you have become too accommodating. Does that mean that you can't be seen as fun or cool to your child or their friends? No. It's just a dangerous line to walk. On a related note, you should not always put your whole trust in other parents' values or ethics unless you know what they are. Just because your child says that the party they will be attending is supervised does not mean that it will be supervised the way you would like to see. Being the cool parent often leads to skirting legal and moral issues so that your child's friends think you're "with it." We knew parents who allowed all the kids who came to their house to smoke, drink, and watch inappropriate movies or video games. You, as your child's protector, need to be aware of what's going on in more than just your own home.

DIANE: *When Chad and Scott were invited to sleepovers, birthday parties, or just to play at someone's house, we needed to know the parents. We checked in with them to get the "whole scoop." As the boys got older they would tell me about the party they'd like to go to, knowing that I would call the parents to see what was going on, who was going* *to be there, ask if they needed help, and mostly make myself aware of the circumstances and confident of the boys' safety. With the first gut instinct of something wrong, I would be that overprotective parent and say no. Sometimes that was actually the answer the boys were looking for, but they didn't want to be the geeks saying no themselves.*

9. Children are a lot like Play-Doh™: When they are young they are moist and easily malleable; they can be shaped into whatever you would like to see. As children get older though and spend more time "outside of their container" they begin to lose some of that moisture; some of their flexibility. At some point (usually just after college) they have been molded into what they will be for the rest of their lives. You want to take as much time when they are young molding them correctly with good values and judgments because the more time you spend forming them while they are young the easier it will be for them to retain their shape as they age.

DIANE: *Imagine yourself in a restaurant with your children. Are they the ones being looked at, smiled at, and complimented? Or are they the ones getting the dirty looks? Do you look at other children and wish* *you could take them home to help them learn how to behave? If this sounds like you, you are probably trying to set limits and manners for your own children. Don't give up on making every situation a learning situation. Because every situation is an opportunity for growth...one way or the other. You are either reinforcing good behavior or reinforcing bad behavior. You get to choose.*

10. Trust is an interesting entity. In the past, people would seal a deal or contract with a simple handshake because trust was given freely in the past; however, in today's world trust is a very rare commodity. Being a person who others feel they can trust is even rarer. In order to set your child apart, to give him or her that trustworthiness, you must start from the time that they are very young and through constant reinforcement and patience urge them to become leaders and stray from the herd.

CHAD: *When I was a little kid, I was kind of a hypochondriac; I was afraid of everything. I learned to face my fears because of a family rule that we had. I don't even know when it was brought up but the rule was, "when either Mom or Dad said 'trust me' you would do what they said without question,"* *because they would never let anything bad happen to you. The term "trust me" became a family motto; I continue to use it to this day, and you will never hear me say "trust me" unless I am one hundred percent sure what the outcome will be.*

MYTH 9

DON'T WORRY, THEY'LL SAY IT AGAIN

How many times have you had to tell your children to do something more than once before they snapped to it? Is it infuriating to know that they aren't listening to you? It should be! When children are very young, we, as parents and teachers, repeat ourselves in order to make sure that our children understand us. Kids learn very early the patterns that make up the world around them, and if a particular pattern states that authority figures will say things more than once if it's really important, then there is no reason to listen the first time around. The problem is the conditioning that we teach our children. When they are very young and their safety is at stake, we do not make time to say things again. When the kids don't listen the first time, they are scolded or punished because we are trying to make a point that their safety is a priority. The trouble comes when we begin to believe that this priority is less important just because it is not an imminent danger situation. The bottom line is that not listening the first time is detrimental to their success.

1. Kids need to learn that they must listen the first time—no more repeating.

2. Children being "in the middle of something" is not an excuse.

3. Have a signal—whistle.

4. Little need for yelling when eye contact, eye level, and emphasis are used.

5. Making others repeat themselves is a sign of disrespect.

6. Listening and understanding can keep you out of danger - safety issue.

7. "I don't get it" is not a question - it's stalling.

8. Parent excuses for repeating - easier, but is it what's best for your child?

9. Learn to notice if they are being dismissive or are appropriately understanding.

1. When safety is an issue we, as parents and teachers, have no problem expressing how vitally important it is to listen the first time around. What we must do now is to impress upon our children that this is always the case and that there is never an excuse for not listening to someone of authority the first time they say anything. Because when you stop to think about it, safety is the goal whether they are 5 or 35. In today's world, where children thrive by disconnecting through the use of cell phones, iPods, and other technological advancements, the human connection of communication is becoming a lost art form that must not be allowed to perish.

CHAD: *The school that I work in currently does not have a policy that outlaws the use of personal music devices such as iPods. Students have become so used to filtering information that they are able (albeit not so well) to listen to someone while leaving their ear buds in their ears with the music still playing. The terrific ability to multitask is wonderful but only if it can be put to good use. The problem that we run into is that students in today's world are inundated with constant input and their brains naturally filter things out. We must be careful not to allow their* *brains to filter out the voice of authority. Children need to learn that the filter they possess works only one direction ...when authority is talking, everything else must be put on hold.*

2. We've all seen the commercials on TV that show a wife trying to talk to her husband while the big game is on and he is shown to have a severe case of "selective hearing." When it's two adults trying to communicate, it may be seen as humorous; however, when that same scene is replayed with children playing video games, it becomes a much more important issue. Children have seen ads like this since before they can remember, and these images take hold of their subconscious unless you are able to show them that it is not how the real world works. Children should absolutely under no circumstances be too busy to listen to what an authority figure has to say. That is not to say that they cannot ask to finish what they are working on, but there MUST be that acknowledgement that they have not only heard you but understood what you were saying.

DIANE: *From the time Chad and Scott were small, dinnertime was dinnertime – no ifs, ands, or buts. They might be playing an exciting video game* *(hunting ducks, usually) very concerned about what level they had reached. If I said, "Time for dinner!" their immediate response had to be "Okay." They were allowed to ask a qualifying question but only after agreeing. Therefore, they would usually say something like, "Okay, but can we please just finish this level?" Then, because they were following the rules, they might get a little longer time before coming to dinner. It would not work, however, if instead of waiting for that answer they assumed they could continue their game. You, as the parent, must always keep the power and require the actions that you want. This plan totally makes your family life happier and calmer.*

3. No matter how well you have done your job as a parent or teacher, there will undoubtedly come a time when you need to make sure that there is no chance of a misunderstanding, or "not hearing." At this point a signal of some sort may be your best remedy. This is any technique or trait that will call full attention; it can be anything from a whistle to an air horn, but it must command the full attention and respect of the children for it to be effective. This again can be used to monitor safety,

or simply draw attention back to the task at hand. One of the most useful places to work on this is in a very public place, but this conditioning must be done at a young age.

CHAD: *When Scott and I were younger, we were constantly active and moving around. We were constantly "exploring," even if it was a place we had been before, like the mall. My dad had a horribly loud whistle that he could do with his lips alone, and anytime we heard that whistle we knew we must be sprinting to Dad without hesitation. This was drilled into us from the time we were very young, and it only took filtering out the whistle and its immediate consequence to make sure that it never happened again. What was the consequence? It would completely depend upon how many times we had made the same mistake before, but I can tell you that it was definitely cumulative!!*

4. As we have stated before, yelling is your least effective way to bring about permanent change. This too goes for helping kids to listen more carefully. Yelling at them when they, "did not hear you" or when they were not paying attention makes your point to no one but you. Does it make you feel a little less helpless? Yes. However,

does it help them fix the problem for next time? No. Eye contact is probably the single best tool for gauging their understanding of what you have said. It is much harder not to listen to someone when you are looking them in the face—harder still when that person is looking for signs of comprehension in your face while talking. Eye level is important as well; children are so used to adults talking "over their head" both figuratively and literally. To get down on one knee and truly talk face to face with your child is so important.

DIANE: *In schools, you can see how children respond in different ways to different types of teachers. One teacher may yell in a child's face. You can see that child get angry as his face freezes in place. At that moment, he cannot listen! His emotions are in that "fight or flight" mode and nothing being said will register. Another teacher will slow down, speak so softly the child must actually lean forward to hear, and calmly discuss the transgression, asking for the child's input. In the second case, the child is far more likely to learn something that he can use in the future because his physiological need to run is no longer being triggered.*

5. Probably the biggest problem with children who do not listen well is that they grow up to be adults who do not listen well. In some cultures, it is the greatest sign of disrespect to make people repeat themselves, and at one time in American history, it was the same here as well. This trend has begun to diminish in recent history. It has gotten so bad lately that kids have started saying "What?" and then saying shortly after, "Oh yeah, yeah. I got it," because they did not give themselves time to understand before asking for clarification.

The act of asking "what," even though you have heard what was said, is a stall tactic by the brain to process the information and decide whether or not it was absorbed. A person who does not listen to those around him is one who does not care about others as much as he cares about himself. What is amazing about our society is that we truly believe that if our students don't learn a skill while they are young, they will pick it up further down the line. In fact, this is completely opposite from the way our brains are structured. If we do not learn a skill while we are young and malleable, we become rigid and unable to acquire new skill sets.

DIANE: *Kids are programmed to say, "What?" from*

the time they are little, so correcting from that time is the easy way. If I said something when the boys were young and they responded with "What?" I could see their eyes turned away from me and their attention on their toys, so I would get down on their level and look in their eyes and say "What do you think I said?" They either already knew or they didn't, but they could tell from my response to their "What?" that it wasn't acceptable. It didn't take many repetitions of this process before they learned to listen the first time. If you're trying to correct that behavior when kids are older, you can try what I often did with kids at school. Fourth, fifth, or sixth graders often say "What?" just to keep from engaging or to give themselves time to think of an answer to your question. Sometimes you can just stare at them quietly and they'll say "Oh!" and respond to what you asked. But sometimes you use the same techniques used with the little guys. You respond to "What?" with "What did I say?" using your game face so they know you're serious about wanting an answer. They will begin to listen more carefully whether that technique is used on them or their classmates.

6. If you happen to be walking along the riverside sometime and notice a child playing on the wrong side of the railing (seconds from falling in) are you going to say something to someone, or are you going to let that child's parents handle their own business? Let's say that same child falls over the railing and drowns because you didn't stop it from happening. Would you be able to live with yourself? The same scenario can be placed upon today's children. We, as parents and teachers, must do everything we can to support our future generations in becoming the best that they are able to be. The fear and anxiety you feel when you see a child doing something that is not safe is the same emotion that you should feel when they decided not to listen to you because not only is their safety in jeopardy, but also their future happiness and success. Seems like a lot to throw on your plate all at once, doesn't it? But this is your role as a parent, or why you have chosen to be a teacher?—to show the guidance that our children need.

> **CHAD:** *At the beginning of the year in my classroom, I talk about how important it is to be respectful and part of that respect is listening to directions the first time. As the year progresses, I find that*

students begin to filter out the latter part of verbal directions, thinking that they can just ask me to repeat it or ask someone near them for clarification. I usually remind the whole class that this behavior is unacceptable and disrespectful and let it go; however, the very next time I see it happening I stop the class and tell everyone that no one in the class is to relay directions to anyone for the rest of the day. If I find out that someone did relay directions both students will be reprimanded (usually just a long talk about respect and honor). This forces the students who were not listening to ask me for clarification, and allows me to talk to them about their not listening without yelling at anyone. Over time my students learn that when I start speaking they need to be paying attention so as not to be reprimanded later.

7. As we talked about earlier, children have a remarkable way of stalling when they do not want to do something. One of the most common phrases that teachers and parents get on a daily basis is "I don't get it." This is not a question, nor is it a true statement, nor does it accomplish anything except the restating of the directions. "I don't get

it" is teenage for "I wasn't listening." Make your children express to you what they "don't get" and what you will find is that they don't get it because they were not fully listening when the directions were given. Make that phrase illegal in your household. Not only will you get kids in the house or classroom who are paying closer attention to what you are saying, but you will also get children who must articulate what they don't understand before they will receive any further help. Now we are working on respect, listening skills, and grammatical prowess all at once. You have to be one step ahead of your child at every turn if you are going to command the respect that authority requires.

CHAD: *It is inevitable that I will have students who are not listening to directions and decide that the best way to figure out how to solve their problem is to raise their hand and say "I don't get it." Most teachers that I know will simply restate the directions because it's easier than trying to prove a point, but I like proving points; it's kind of my "go to" technique. At the beginning of the school year I tell them that "I don't get it" is illegal in my room and that if I hear it, the class will all stop what they are doing and help you to get it! It doesn't take long* *before somebody tests the waters and utters that illegal phrase. To show them that I was serious, I reply "Uh oh—I heard it. Did you guys hear it? Somebody said, 'I don't get it'," and I make the class stop and listen to the student vocalize what he didn't understand. Yes, it's nerve-wracking for the student, but through talking to the class he almost always realize that he did hear what was said and that he is not really confused about anything. It also forces him to formulate an actual question before asking me and the class for help.*

8. "Sometimes isn't it just easier to repeat what I have said instead of fighting the small fight?" The short answer to this question is a resounding, "yes!" However, is it more beneficial for your child's future? Absolutely not. Since we have all come to the agreement that nothing in this world should be more important to you than your children, we must then admit that there is no such thing as a small fight when raising kids is the task. Everything you do affects their upbringing—everything. And for every one time that you back down and change your game plan it takes 20 more attempts at doing it right to correct it in their minds. When people say that being a parent is the hardest job in

the whole world, they are right, assuming that you want the best for your child. If you do not want what's best, parenting can be a breeze. Fortunately this question is asked in the darkest corners of your subconscious. In case you're worried, if you're reading this book, you probably want the best and are doing a great job!

DIANE: *I had a parent during a parenting class bragging about how his plan for getting his child to do anything was great. He said, "I give them three chances to do it. Then I come after them. They know I'll do that so they do what I say." Many parents do the counting thing to get their kids to follow directions, but my question is, "If you could make them do it on the third chance, why not make them do it on the first?" In essence, you're teaching them not to follow through with your directions until the third time (even if you yell) because you don't really care until then. This plan causes an escalation in voice level and irritation for the parent...never a good thing.*

9. Being a step ahead of your children is a technique that takes years to master, but can be used within days of its implementation because it is all about observation. You

must observe your children and learn their habits and mannerisms. Just like in poker, everybody has tells. A tell is a gesture, look, twitch, etc. It's anything that gives other people information about you or what you are thinking. Your children have tells too! Getting to know what these signs are can be your greatest attribute to being their parent. You get to see them more than any other person (and if you don't, you should start now). When children are not listening, they have a completely different body language about them than when they are listening and understanding. Learn to notice the different mannerisms they have and what those mannerisms could mean.

CHAD: *There are many times that I have a student who has "forgotten" their project at home and wants to keep from getting in trouble. I will see these students walking in, laughing and carrying on with their friends. They sit and talk and have no immediate desire to go anywhere until someone notices what has been written on the board: "Have assignment out for Fink check" (my version of a pop quiz). Suddenly, that student's face changes; he looks around nervously and searches frantically through his folder. About the time I am finishing* *attendance, this student comes to me and says that he feels really bad and wants to go to the office. I tell him he absolutely can go and his face brightens for a split second, until I mention that I will need to see his assignment before he leaves. At which point the student slumps and says that he doesn't have it. I then write him a pass to go to the office; sometimes this student shows up to class later with the assignment in hand. Unfortunately for this student, the assignment was already due and can only be counted for late credit. Being able to read this student's body language allowed me to force him to learn a lesson about responsibility that otherwise he might not have learned if I hadn't asked to see the assignment before he left.*

MYTH 10

I HATE FAMILY TIME

Everything that we have talked about not only leads to this final chapter but also starts with this final chapter as well. We have come full circle. Without the family structure in place everything else falls apart. The term "family" is a loose term and for our purposes the terms "parent" and "teacher" are interchangeable because when you truly care about the wellbeing of children, the job description is the same. Most of what we have talked about seems too farfetched to accomplish in the world in which we live, but it is possible. There is nothing in this world that counts as much as family. Choose to make your family structure strong and enduring. Choose to buy stock in your children instead of in the market. Choose to schedule business meetings within your home instead of at work. Choose to give yourself and your family that raise that you all deserve.

1. Don't use terms like "family time"—just make it part of your everyday routine.

2. Your child should ALWAYS be more important to you than business, phone calls, etc.

3. Don't give your children a "play area"—have them play near you.

4. The "Key" is to recognize and interpret expressions.

5. Be one step ahead of your kids at all times.

6. Let the good happen, allow some bad to teach valuable lessons, and prevent the catastrophic all together.

7. Encourage silly play—participate.

8. Time spent together is a voluntary act—choose to make it work.

1. Part of the reason why so many kids hate family time is because of the simple fact that we call it family time - as if it's some kind of forced event. Kids, especially very young kids, don't care what they are doing as long as it is fun for them. What if they grew up and never heard the term "family time," but every time they were with the family they were having fun together? Would that child hate the time spent with family? Of course not. This is the way to ensure that kids not only tolerate but enjoy spending time with the family. It must be fun, and not just fun for the parent—it must be fun for all. Spending quality time with the family is one of the very few commodities in life that does not cost anything to be enjoyed. Make a little time every single day to spend getting to know your kids again because they change a little more every day.

DIANE: *Dinnertime in our family was always spent together, with only minor exceptions. It was a time of giggles and talking. There was no radio or TV, no newspaper or phone. But the best part was that there was no rule against any of this, we just didn't even think of it. Everyone ate together; no one left the table without permission and then only left when everyone was finished. We learned manners and* *other social skills just by being together and enjoying each other's company. We would occasionally have a "picnic" dinner in the family room watching TV or outside on a blanket. If we ate in a restaurant, all rules still applied, manners and courtesy were to be used, but we did have fun together. That should be the point of "family time."*

2. Suffice it to say that we may have mentioned that your children should be the most important thing in your life. With that said, why would you not want to spend as much time with those people as possible? It used to be that when your work day ended you went home and enjoyed your family time for the rest of the evening. This, unfortunately, is no longer the case. In today's technologically "advanced" world, we are only a text message or email away from our work desk. Are there jobs that REQUIRE you to be on call? Absolutely, but before you pigeonhole yourself into thinking that you have one of those jobs, ask yourself honestly, "Would it be possible for me to not answer my phone after work hours?" Most of us will have to answer "Yes, it is at least possible." It is time to break the cycle of work and money coming first and instead turn to a new belief system that has quality time with family at its core.

DIANE: *It was very easy for us as the boys were growing up to keep the distractions away because there weren't as many of them, but the idea remains the same: distractions detract from loving family interaction. If the boys were watching TV, we generally were too—watching the same show on the same TV; sometimes their choice, sometimes ours. They might be playing with toys at the same time, or we could all be cuddling together on the couch. You may think that teenagers don't want that cuddling thing, but yes they do—sometimes more than little ones do. Don't let their attitudes fool you. They still want to know that they are the most important thing in your world. Show them that phone calls or emails can wait until later. You will see a difference in how they respond to you if you show them (not tell them) that they come first.*

3. In keeping with the theme of spending quality time with the family, we must tackle the concept of children's play areas. In most circumstances, the children have an area of the house designated for playing in so that the rest of the house doesn't look cluttered with toys and games. This is kind of like the old plastic couch covers that people

used to use to "protect" their furniture; although they did protect the furniture they also made the house look tacky and unlivable for all of the guests that ever stopped by. Are your possessions or your children more important to you? Because your children will never need replacing, no matter how much the styles or materials change. Create a house that encourages children to remain part of the family; a house that tells people that you are proud to have children despite the occasional stains and toy-strewn living spaces. One of the exciting side effects of this type of family bonding is the ability for parents to remain young at heart. Play with your children at every opportunity because you will be able to teach them more through modeled behavior and hands-on learning than you ever imagined.

> **CHAD:** *My brother and I were diehard soccer players growing up, and on rainy days when playing in the yard was out of the question, we often moved our games indoors. Because we grew up in a household where play was encouraged we would sometimes play in areas that were, looking back on it, very poor choices. There were more than a couple occasions in which a lampshade was broken, or a window was*

cracked despite using soft indoor balls. We were scolded and we were made to pay for replacement of anything we broke, but even that taught us lessons about responsibility and positive decision making. More than anything though, we learned that our parents were not worried about their physical possessions as much as they were that we had our family time together.

4. Each child is an individual: they all have similar features and mannerisms such as smiling when happy and crying when sad. However, it is the subtle differences in between that make your child unique. It is in these subtle differences that you can truly learn who your child really is. The best technique that you, as a parent or teacher, can possess is the ability to "read" your children. These micro-emotional signals are the windows to our souls. Being able to see and interpret what your children are thinking or feeling without them telling you is such an important facet in the parent /child dynamic. There are many times that children are afraid to let you know what they are thinking or what they are afraid of because they believe that either you will not understand or that you will be angry that what they are scared of is something that

you might consider trivial. Watch your children the way babies watch their surroundings. Don't just look at your children;- see them. Each child will show you who he is on a daily basis as long as you know what to look for, and because each child's micro-emotional signals are different, it is up to you to learn who they are as individuals.

CHAD: *Each and every fall I have a new batch of students who breeze through my doors with no idea what to expect from me. Inevitably, by the end of the year though, all of my students have learned my body language and non-verbal signals. When I cross my arms and raise one eyebrow, they know that I am waiting and will not tolerate much more before a consequence is imposed. They also know when I smirk and shake my head back and forth that I may agree that what they are saying is funny or amusing, but that I am not going to encourage it to continue and interrupt instruction time. And even though I have 180 new faces per year, I pride myself on being able to read my students as well as or better than anyone else in my educational circle. Most people are able to recognize that less than 10 percent of human communication is verbal; over 90 percent* *is body language and subtle micro-emotional cues. Learning to read those cues can make a world of difference in your relationship with your children.*

5. Once you start to learn what your children are thinking based on their micro signs, the next step is to be able to read the onset of those signs. You should always know where your children are, what they are doing and how they are feeling at all times. This may sound like an impossibility, but in fact it just takes some time, practice, and communication. When your kids are about to ask you for something, you should already know the signs they are giving you. These signs will help you to make your decision even before the child asks the question. If they happen to be giving you the guilty look when asking to visit a friend's house for a party, there's a good chance that they may not be telling you everything. When they come up to you and ask the same question with confidence while looking you in the eye, there is a good chance that they have told you everything that they know about the situation. If you are caught off-guard by your children in either of these situations, either because you are too busy or because you do not know their mannerisms closely enough, you will not be able to interpret their signs in

time to make an informed decision.

DIANE: *When you can "read" your kids, you can adjust their behavior before it becomes inappropriate. I would ask Chad and Scott if they had picked up the toys in the basement, and because of slight looks they didn't know they were giving, I could quickly say, "Why don't you check it out to make sure?" They would hurriedly go finish the job, and no one had to be in trouble because of not doing a chore, or more importantly, for telling a lie about it. Catching them in a lie is not the option you are looking for. What you want is to keep them from telling the lie in the first place. So always be aware of what their expressions are telling you so that you can redirect both their behavior and their verbal responses to you.*

6. As a parent or teacher, your goal is to provide guidance for your children; to give them insight and protection, but to allow them to learn the lessons that will make them the productive self-assured members of society that you hope for. One of the major problems that today's parents face is deciding what should be a life lesson and what should be prevented. Unfortunately, the parents of the past did

such a great job of scaring their children that many of today's parents believe that everything negative should be prevented, no matter the cost. Children need to learn lessons in order to grow. Yes, there are catastrophic events that parents should keep their children from experiencing if at all possible, but doing poorly on a school assignment because it was left at home is not catastrophic, nor is anything of the like. Catastrophic is anything that can permanently damage their psyches or stigmatize (their minds or their viewpoints) or is just plain dangerous. Things like continued bullying should not be tolerated, but your child should be given the chance to fix it for him or herself before you fix it for them. Jumping in the lake without a life jacket is obviously not the time to let them experience failure, but we must try not to solve every problem our children may have. They need to know that they can persevere and solve their own problems.

CHAD: *When I was in fourth grade, I decided that I wanted to do something crazy with my hair. It was a time when "steps" (the shaved lines in your hair just above your ears) were in fashion. My dad used to cut my hair for me instead of going to a barber, and I begged him to cut these steps into my hair.*

He was leery about doing it because he knew I would freak out when I saw it, but he just asked me one more time if I was sure. I said, "Yes," and the next thing I knew, I was looking in the mirror and crying because the steps didn't look like what I had envisioned. He felt terrible but allowed me to choose my own path; he allowed me to experience a little disappointment and a little failure in order to help me grow. That haircut is still, to this day, one of my absolute favorites because I proved to myself that I could do something out of the ordinary and get through it on my own.

7. Childhood is short and anything that you can do as a parent or teacher to prolong this time is important. Remember when you were a kid and all you wanted to do was grow up? You used to want to be so mature; you emulated everyone around you that you admired. As you grew up, you became that mature and older person you always wanted to be…and then you missed the child you used to be. Being young is amazing and fun and interesting, so keep it that way, not only for your child but for the inner child you miss from time to time. Being silly with the family is what life is all about. Encourage your

children to be silly and to embrace being young because as you know all too well, childhood is gone before you know it. Why do you think we go through mid-life crises?! You need to remember what being a kid is like and how to incorporate that into your teaching methods used with your children.

DIANE: *If it sounds like we were always good role models—nope, not true! There were times that what we did as a family might have been slightly inappropriate (at least to some people), but it built great family memories. In restaurants, we would sometimes have saltshaker wars. Each person would slide the shaker to the opposite side of the table trying to get it as close to the edge as possible without falling off. There was no scorekeeping, no yelling, no huge competition—just family fun while we were waiting for the food to be served. Riding bikes in the rain and coming home with a mud streak up the middle of your back and having your parents encourage you to have that fun worked because the boys asked if it was okay beforehand. That meant the clothes and timing were acceptable. Have fun!! Finger paint, use clay (make your own),* *cook with your kids, play "hot hands," hang spoons from your nose, play games in the car...interact with one another... join the party!!*

8. Family time is what you choose to make of it. It can be something to be dreaded or it can be the best part of your life; the reason you get out of bed in the morning. Choosing your family over all of the other "distractions" in your life is the single greatest gift you can give to yourself and your family members. Choose to make life worth living. Choose to make your family your priority. Once you make this choice, the parenting style that you are searching for will develop naturally and your life will take on a whole new meaning. To live for those you love is selfless, and this selflessness is what will teach you how to parent or teach in the most effective way possible. Good luck and best wishes!!

THANK YOU

Thank you for reading our collection of tips and techniques for parents and educators to use to guide a child's behavior. We hope you have found at least one of these tips to help your children to enhance their ability to more easily become independent, successful adults.

Please visit us on our website and blog at:
http://childhoodmyths.net

We wish you well! Happy parenting!

D & C

Made in the USA
Lexington, KY
26 June 2011